Privilege, Risk, and Solidarity

Privilege, Risk, and Solidarity

Understanding Undocumented Immigration through Feminist Christian Ethics

Libby Mae Grammer

WIPF & STOCK · Eugene, Oregon

PRIVILEGE, RISK, AND SOLIDARITY
Understanding Undocumented Immigration through Feminist Christian
Ethics

Wipf & Stock
An Imprint of Wipf and Stock Publishers
199 W. 8th Ave., Suite 3
Eugene, OR 97401

www.wipfandstock.com

PAPERBACK ISBN: 978-1-5326-0682-3
HARDCOVER ISBN: 978-1-5326-0684-7
EBOOK ISBN: 978-1-5326-0683-0

Manufactured in the U.S.A.   FEBRUARY 21, 2017

This book is dedicated to the millions of undocumented immigrants who live among us and yet have no voice, and to Christian and secular feminists before me who have opened our eyes to oppression, given voice to the voiceless, and taken enormous risks to stand in solidarity with the marginalized. May we all find inspiration and challenge as we explore how best to live among our neighbors as God intended.

Contents

Acknowledgments

THIS BOOK WOULD NOT be possible without the dedication of friends and colleagues who love to edit (looking at you, Heather Renae Gentry, Dr. Bert Browning, and Dr. Bob Dale), professors who guided me in my exploration of Christian Ethics and Academic Research (looking at you, Dr. David Gushee, Dr. Larry McSwain, Dr. Nancy L. Declaisse-Walford, Dr. Margaret Mohrmann, and Dr. Charles Mathewes), a dear family who has loved and supported me through my educational and faith journeys (looking at you, William Underwood, Brenda & Rick Grammer, and Lynne Grammer Mashburn), and a deeply important nearly ten-year period of growth and legal education in my first professional job as an immigration paralegal with a spectacular attorney and friend in Chattanooga, TN (looking at you, Robert C. Divine).

Thanks.

Introduction

YOU MIGHT APPROACH THIS book with a few questions in your mind: What is feminist ethics, really? Who are undocumented immigrants? How could these two topics possibly have anything to do with one another? Bringing together the tenants of feminism, especially those legacies in Black feminist liberationist theology, Womanist theology, and *Mujerista* theology, with the issues and lives of marginalized undocumented immigrants makes sense. This is because feminism is a movement spawned by strong women, marginalized by deeply patriarchal cultures, and un-documented immigrants lead similar lives of marginalization and oppression under current U.S. immigration policy and U.S. social culture, which are composed of systemic racism and xenophobia. Additionally, the work of feminists for decades of scholarship has allowed the voices of women and many other marginalized people to be heard in the public sphere. So, whether you are an academic researching issues through different theological lenses or a layperson trying to understand the deeply complex legal and theological world of undocumented immigration, this book can provide some aid to grasp some of the basic concepts so that we may all better understand this issue, as told from the margins.

Foremost, feminism *listens* as much as it tells. It listens to the historically left-out groups.[1] In its best forms, it halts the speech

---

1. Though feminism is not without its flaws. We will explore later in the

of those who would drown out minority voices. It draws up those who are bent down by oppression. Feminism to me is simply good Christianity. A study of scripture—from its narratives and mandates—also opens a wide variety of stories in our own sacred tradition that listens to the voice of the least and the last. This kind of scriptural study in the midst of listening to the most unheard comes naturally for me, a Baptist with high regard for the stories of God's love by those faithful who have come before. And more than that, as a woman who came from a rather conservative background that did not support my ordination or pastoral ministry, my story in its own small way resonates with those left out. When I begin to see my own oppressors and their blindness to their own prejudices, I also begin to see my own complicity and privilege among those with even less of a voice in this world. This is what I believe Jesus was saying when he wanted his followers to see the Son of God in the person with no home, the person in prison, the stranger in your midst, or the person with no food or clothing.[2] Pay attention. *See.* Hear the voices speak their own truths about their lives rather than trying to speak it for them. Learn, and grow alongside people on the margins. This is how to be a follower of God in this world.

Feminist theology and ethics reminds me to be this kind of follower of Jesus, and its implications run far and deep in my life. For almost a decade, I have spent many hours assisting immigration clients with their paperwork, and while most of it was typical corporate immigration work, some family-based cases reached into my soul and reminded me that for every visa application I filled out, for every hardship application sent in, there was a story and a life of migration, change, and hospitality (or lack thereof). Who would I be in this world? Would I be the person that put myself and my own interests first, assuming that if I did not think

book how feminism began as largely a white, wealthy, female phenomenon. Thankfully, with time and lots more listening, feminism is beginning to listen to a wider range of female voices, including our Black liberationist sisters, our Womanist sisters, and our *Mujerista* sisters.

2. Matt 25:35–40. All Scripture quoted is from the NRSV, unless otherwise indicated.

I had done anything wrong that obviously I had not? Or would I stop to hear how my daily living might be causing someone else harm? Would I then act in solidarity to improve the lots of those whose lives are precious, but who have been bent down in fear for too long? Or would I cower away in guilt and say and do nothing? My whiteness and my U.S. citizenship limits me in so many ways when it comes to issues which do not harm me personally. How can I begin to write about an issue when I have no first-hand experience? I have never emigrated anywhere. My five month study abroad in college notwithstanding, I have not even truly lived abroad. Who am I to speak of these issues? True, I have spent a good deal of time in study, but more than any theory of justice, or more than any explanation of problems with laws, the truth is in stories. As we seek to understand feminist ethics, to understand immigration law, to explore the foundations of a way to be Christian that calls us to a radical way of life, I hope this book also gives space and voice to the lives most impacted by structural problems leading to their oppression, even as it challenges those of us who have the privilege in this country to call for change.

What is Feminist Ethics?

Christian feminist ethics is a subset of the larger philosophy and movement known as feminism. Functioning at its most base form, it represents a fundamental belief that gender discrimination should be identified and opposed. Sexism in society—whether individual or structural—has led feminists to oppose "gendered patterns of domination and subordination, gendered role differentiation, gender-biased unequal access to goods and services."[3] Feminist ethics, then, is the study of the practices that seek equality of respect and recognition of personhood regardless of gender. Feminist ethics takes into account the well-being and experience of real women rather than simply seeking universal principles alone (but without discounting the importance of some guiding

---

3. Farley, "Feminist Ethics," 5.

and universal principles across cultural lines). Feminism seeks to take particularity and universality and work them into a cohesive ethical reflection that focuses on the autonomy, equality, and mutuality of women and women's experience. Feminist theology, in much the same way, critiques religious practices and beliefs that exalt the attributes of men while subordinating the role of women. This work of seeking mutuality and equality in the midst of seeking the autonomy of women has led Christian feminist ethicists to seek justice for any oppressed or marginalized group, addressing issues of responsibility, violence, class, ethnicity, power, and societal change.

In other words, feminist thought and theology does not exist solely to speak to "women's issues." To be sure, feminism was borne of the need for women's voices to be heard, as they were marginalized and excluded from public and academic discourse. But ultimately, feminism, and its more specific voices in Black Feminist Liberationist theology, *Mujerista* theology, and Womanist theology all are pointing out weaknesses in our academically privileged discourse; namely, that we often ignore and marginalize those who hold little power in a society dominated by white, male power structures—women, minorities, those with minority sexual orientations, and any others who do not conform to male and heteronormative ideals that are entrenched in our culture.

Feminist theology and ethics takes into account various categories and contextualization to better understand the realities of social injustices. From the goals of seeking to recognize the personhood and embodied nature of all individuals to the idea that human beings are intrinsically connected through shared stories in community, feminist ethics asks about the whole of our being as humans, and thus reaches beyond mere *theories* of justice and into the lives and stories of the marginalized people themselves. Feminism is thus more than identity politics, setting women's interests above that of other groups (read: feminism is not just about man-hating or seeking a matriarchal society). No, feminist ethics is part of a systematic thought process that involves the addressing of hierarchical structures while seeking to shift how we all see the world around us. This new "way of seeing" provides a new point of view to both the privileged and the marginalized, re-telling the narratives we take for granted based on our social locations, ultimately leading to better understanding, more open dialogue, and the hope for changes to better support one another in our shared humanity.

Why Feminism for Undocumented Immigration?

As we explore the timely and important issue of undocumented immigration, one might ask—why feminism? While feminist theology is not the only effective theology to employ to approach this issue,[4] it does offer specific perspectives that help Christians in ways other theologies may fall short. Feminist literature provides valuable insight for Christians trying to understand how to approach the issue of undocumented immigration by revealing the worth of the marginalized and listening to them. It also indicates to the privileged their shortcomings and aids them in finding new ways to interact with the marginalized that improve everyone's lots (and souls). Specifically, feminist theology does three important things:

- It supports the cause of immigration reform through its emphases on giving voice to the marginalized;

- It recognizes the autonomy of the marginalized; and

- In doing the first two, it teaches the privileged how to stand in solidarity with the marginalized.

---

4. Virtue ethics, deontological consequentialism, liberation theology, and even biblical literalism, have all been used to support arguments for immigration reform (and some have been used against reform as well). I argue that where these fall short in their arguments for reforming immigration laws to aid those most marginalized—the undocumented—is their lack of attention to the voices of the marginalized and/or their lack of attention to how the privileged can help in ways that do not overpower the autonomy of marginalized people. Feminist theology and ethics deals with these specific issues in helpful ways, as we will explore here.

In this book, then, we will explore all of these avenues and then offer some concrete approaches for focusing Christian energies into the good work of welcoming those around us into our tradition and society in better ways than we have in the past. These will include ways to advocate politically and ways to serve one another individually and in church communities. In chapter one, "Learning the Experience," we explore a brief history of U.S. immigration to provide a frame of reference, including outlining many of the important legal decisions about immigration of the last century and examining the legal shortfalls in detail. Chapter two, "Telling the Stories, Part I," examines the importance of story for Christians, beginning with biblical exegesis of relevant immigrant passages in the Old and New Testaments. Chapter three, "Telling the Stories, Part II," then frames the importance of story within Black Feminist Liberationist and *Mujerista* theology, followed by outlining the stories and lives of real immigrants and the social and legal predicaments they find themselves in due to outdated immigration laws. Chapter four, "Recognizing the Realities," goes on to provide a Womanist understanding of culturally-produced evil and explores further how the U.S. legal system is steeped in systemic injustice for the marginalized. This chapter also includes a frank look at what it means to have white, U.S. Citizen privilege and what it means to be marginalized. Chapter five, "Responding Appropriately," gives ways in which feminist theology can aid in a comprehensive Christian response to this issue, including a thorough understanding of the need to see and listen (based on a review of various sources, incl. *Ana Maria Isasi-Díaz, Traci West, Emilie Townes*, etc.); the need for responsibility and autonomy for the marginalized (incl. secular feminist *Martha Nussbaum*); and the importance of risk taking (incl. *Sharon Welch*) and solidarity (incl. *Rebecca Todd Peters*).

1

Learning the Experience

AMERICANS CONSISTENTLY GATHER INFORMATION related to the topic of United States immigration through news networks and viral internet rumors, including recent outright falsehoods politicians and news programming report as truth. For instance, the presidential campaign for President Donald Trump insisted time and again that Mexico is "sending the bad ones over"[1]—suggesting that only criminals are crossing the border, leaving the United States bombarded with upwards of 30 million (note: there are approximately 11 million)[2] unauthorized and mostly dangerous immigrants.[3] These constant barrages of partial-and non-truths can often lead to misinformation and enflamed passion from those who choose to look no further than media-driven political soundbites. Far right-wing political forces in this country have begun to lean sharply toward a deportation and enforcement-only culture that

1. Jacobson, "Donald Trump: 'The Mexican government . . . they send the bad ones over.'"

2. Sherman, "Donald Trump wrongly says the number of illegal immigrants is 30 million or higher."

3. Whether or how the new Trump administration will follow through on campaign promises to deport millions of undocumented immigrants, insist on registration for all Muslim-Americans, build a costly wall at the Mexican-American border, or require Congress to pass laws ensuring lowered immigration from countries with ties to ISIS, remains to be seen. The 2016 election results have left palpable fear among minorities and the undocumented.

seeks to homogenize American culture and undo the immigrant effects of changing culture. The party base for the Tea Party and increasingly, the mainstream Republican party, are largely white and support mass deportation or some derivation of that policy, including registration of certain minorities simply for their faith tradition; and further, they want leaders who consistently speak up against any further immigration to the United States, especially from Mexico or Arab-speaking countries/Muslim immigrants.[4] While a few conservative lawmakers and politicians have called for a more welcoming immigration policy,[5] the deepening divide between Democrats and Republicans, along with a sensationalist media-driven push toward extremism, has left us with an elected Congress that remains in a stalemate, unable to make but a few positive and bipartisan decisions.

In light of so much false information saturating the last decade of ever-widening polarization of American politics, U.S. Christians must look beyond the political editorializing and into the facts and real-life stories of undocumented immigration in the United States today.[6] For Christians who take seriously the claims in Scripture to love the stranger and practice hospitality, the reality of over 11 million undocumented persons living within our borders on the farthest margins of society, with no access to social resources and without a voice to defend themselves, creates a very real theological and ethical problem with which to grapple. The problem of undocumented immigration forces U.S. citizen (especially privileged, white) Christians, to face an ever-present human issue. This requires deep introspection about their own privilege[7]

4. Bacon, "Trump Supporters Deeply Wary of Illegal Immigration, Syrian Refugees in the U.S.: Polls."

5. Altman, "In Historic Vote, Senate Passes Historic Bipartisan Immigration Bill."

6. For more answers to questions posed by the editorializing of sensationalist journalism and politics, the American Immigration Council's Immigration Policy Center has compiled a list of comprehensive answers to frequent questions raised about immigration on their website: "Giving the Facts a Fighting Chance."

7. As will be discussed later in this work, privilege must be recognized by

as citizens as well as spiritual conviction about, and thoughtful analysis of, this problem from a place of solidarity, responsibility, and mutual love.

To explore how Christians can respond faithfully to this issue to the ends mentioned above, many types of ethical methodology have been used. Virtue ethics, deontological consequentialism, liberation theology, and even biblical literalism, have all been used to support arguments for immigration reform (and some have been used against reform as well). Where these fall short in their arguments for reforming immigration laws to aid those most marginalized—the undocumented—is their lack of attention to the voices of the marginalized and/or their lack of attention to how the privileged can help in ways that do not overpower the autonomy of marginalized people. Feminist theology and ethics deal with these specific issues, providing a plethora of tools with which to approach issues of social importance in deeper, more meaningful ways. The work of feminist ethicists (both Christian and secular) has been developed in scholarship for decades, and its function should not be to simply support or erase other methodologies, but to provide a new method of imagining ethical dilemmas. These new approaches to ethics focus on listening to the voices of those most often left out of the equations in methodologies focused on solving problems, and instead hear deliberately the voices of those affected by the ethical issues raised. To be sure, no methodology will provide the answer to all of the questions in a given social issue, but methodologies that listen to those affected will most fully reflect the work of Christ, who listened, taught, and lived among people of all walks of life. This book will look at the realities of undocumented immigration while exploring a subset of the scholarship of Christian (and some secular) feminist ethicists because the methodologies within these works can be applied to important

---

those who hold it. Doing this entails first-world (or in this case, U.S. citizen—especially Caucasian) persons recognizing their own responsibility, complicity, and privilege in relation to those on the margins of their society, including and especially those without proper legal immigration status. See Peters, *Solidarity Ethics*, 38ff.

aspects of undocumented U.S. immigration as a political and social problem.

As mentioned in the introduction, feminist literature provides valuable insight for Christians trying to understand how to approach the issue of undocumented immigration. It affirms the worth of the marginalized and listens to them, and it indicates to the privileged their shortcomings and aids them in finding new ways to interact with the marginalized that improve everyone's lots (and souls). Specifically, feminist theology does three important things:

1. It supports the cause of immigration reform through its emphases on giving voice to the marginalized;

2. It recognizes the autonomy of the marginalized; and

3. In doing the first two, it teaches the privileged how to stand in solidarity with the marginalized.

Who are Undocumented Immigrants?

Before exploring the biblical and feminist scholarship on this issue, it is helpful to know a little about those persons the U.S. immigration system labels "undocumented" or "unauthorized" immigrants."[8] Undocumented (or unauthorized) immigrants are those persons present in the United States without proper immigrant or nonimmigrant[9] status, as authorized by the U.S.

---

8. Note that while U.S. immigration law does use the term "alien" as a technical term for foreign nationals, this term has fallen out of use in academic circles due to its use by anti-immigrant groups as a slur that dehumanizes a large swath of the U.S. population. For purposes of this work, I will interchangeably use "undocumented immigrants" and "unauthorized immigrants" as descriptive only of the immigrant's lack of legal immigration status, not as a descriptor of their personhood or worth.

9. Immigrants are those persons seeking to live long-term or permanently in the United States. Nonimmigrants are those who enter the U.S. for short term purposes (visiting, studying, or working). Those without status may have entered legally and then overstayed their allotted time in the U.S. and now no longer have legal status, or they may have sneaked across the U.S. border, never

Citizenship and Immigration Services (USCIS) of the Department of Homeland Security (DHS). The realities of the sheer scope of the marginalization of huge groups of people are one place to begin to understand the problem at hand. Thus, we begin by studying the facts surrounding those that current U.S. law deems "undocumented."

Statistics

According to the Pew Research Center, there were approximately 11.2 million unauthorized immigrants in the U.S. as of the year 2012, a number that has not changed much since 2009. Before that time, U.S. undocumented immigration had been rising rapidly, peaking at 12.2 million in 2007, the beginning of the Great Recession.[10] Undocumented immigrants are overwhelmingly Latino/a, with over 8.8 million of the 11.2 million undocumented coming from Latin America. Of these, 7 million are of Mexican heritage.[11] To contrast with these numbers, the overwhelming majority of foreign-born persons in the U.S. have legal immigration status (temporary/nonimmigrant status or permanent residence). There are approximately 40.4 million foreign-born persons present in the U.S., fewer than 30% of whom currently have no legal immigration status.[12]

In 2008, there were 6.3 million men, 4.1 million women, and 1.5 million children under age 18 living as undocumented immigrants in the U.S. Three quarters of households headed by unauthorized immigrants are married or cohabiting couples with or without children. Notwithstanding the abundance of young men (35% of unauthorized immigrants are men age 18–29, compared with only 14% among U.S.-born population), the majority of unauthorized immigrants live in the U.S. with their family. Nearly half

having held any legal immigration status.

10. Passel and Cohn, "A Portrait of Unauthorized Immigrants."

11. Passel and Cohn, "Origins of Unauthorized Immigrants."

12. Pew Hispanic Research Center, "Data Trend—Society and Demographics, Immigrants."

of all unauthorized family heads are living with both a spouse and children under age 18 (48%). Many families are "mixed-status," or families with unauthorized immigrants and their U.S. citizen children or legal resident family members. In this group, 3.8 million are unauthorized immigrant adults and half a million are unauthorized immigrant children. The U.S. citizens (mostly children) and the legal immigrant family members make up the rest. The information from the Pew Center states that "Since 2003, the number of children (both U.S. born and unauthorized) in these mixed-status families has increased to 4.5 million from 3.3 million. This increase is attributable almost entirely to the increasing number of U.S. citizen children living with undocumented parents."[13]

The 2007 median income for undocumented immigrants was $36,000 per year, which is well below the mean of $50,000 per year for U.S.-born persons. The income of undocumented immigrants, as compared with that of other legal-status immigrants and American citizens on the whole, does not increase significantly the longer they live in the United States. According to the Pew Center's research, "a third of the children of unauthorized immigrants and a fifth of adult unauthorized immigrants live in poverty. This is nearly double the poverty rate for children of U.S.-born parents (18%) or for U.S.-born adults (10%)."[14] Thus, unauthorized immigrants are not only unrepresented in the country where they live, a large number of them are living at or below the poverty line with their families and receive little to no government support.

U.S. undocumented immigration is a particularly human issue because it involves vulnerable humans seeking to improve their lot in life; but the issue is particularly relevant and appropriate to the field of Christian feminist ethics because of its focus on the plight of the marginalized and oppressed, its resolution requiring attendance to systemic issues of injustice through reform of immigration laws. Oppression of the undocumented comes in multiple forms, such as lack of access to representation in government, low wage earnings at often back-breaking jobs with no recourse to

13. Passel and Cohn, "Demographic and Family Characteristics."
14. Passel and Cohn, "A Portrait of Unauthorized Immigrants."

government assistance or worker's rights, lack of access to health insurance,[15] lack of access to basic identification documents due to some state laws barring all undocumented immigrants from obtaining legal state ID or driver's licenses,[16] and an ongoing fear of deportation and family separation.[17] Undocumented immigrants are some of the most socially and politically marginalized persons in the United States, and their plight warrants the attention of Christians who care about social justice and making social and political changes to improve the life circumstances of others, their neighbors created in the image of God.

Additionally, feminist ethics focuses strongly on recognizing the structures and systems behind such oppression. Whether it is Martha Nussbaum's capabilities approach, emphasizing autonomy and equal regard, Traci West's liberationist feminist thought, stressing the conditions that ensnare the socially marginalized, Emilie Townes' Womanist approach to the ways culture can produce evil, or Ana Maria Isasi-Díaz's *Mujerista* stories and emotive moves toward change, feminist ethics (especially Christian feminist ethics) has much to say to human issues involving systems of oppression and the struggles of the marginalized, as well as to those who do the oppressing and benefit from such structures. We will explore these perspectives in more detail in the following chapters, along with some ways in which they can speak directly to the specific issue of undocumented immigration.

15. Ibid.

16. Only about ten states will issue driver's licenses to undocumented immigrants, including most recently, California. Berman, "California Begins Issuing Driver's Licenses Regardless of Immigration Status."

17. U.S. deportation of undocumented immigrants reached an all-time high in 2013, the fifth year of the Obama administration, which had campaigned on promises of immigration reform and has only in the last year begun the process of reining in deportations of non-criminals and young people brought illegally into the country as young children: Pew Hispanic Research Center, "Unauthorized Immigrants."

A Brief Modern History of
Undocumented Immigration

Christians must first become informed, do research, and learn the historical and legal realities of immigration and its history in the United States to fully grasp the problems at hand. Most people recognize that the United States, a nation founded by immigrants, has long been viewed by other nations as inherently welcoming. Made up of largely European immigrants seeking new lives, the country faced the struggle throughout the years to begin deciding who was worthy to be admitted into the union and who was not.[18] The freedom given to those foreigners who came to the United States once the country was founded was limited, even from the earliest Asian workers, to enslaved Africans, forced by their fellow humanity to emigrate to the new nation.[19] So this trend continues, in varying ways, even as the country has grown into a more tolerant society. Worries about who these "others" are and why they come, along with the ongoing fears associated with cultures that appear different than mainstream American culture, leave the political process paralyzed.

Immigration has a long and complex history, especially beginning in the twentieth century. After World War I, the country began to seek to limit immigration in ways it had not sought in previous centuries. The Immigration Act of 1924 was the culmination of the fears and desires of a nation struggling with a more globally-connected world. The act limited the number of

18. While the focus of this book will be on the United States immigration system and Christian responses to it, we wish to also give voice to those oppressed by the forcible taking of this land by European immigrants. The Native Americans are those to whom those of us of other origins in the U.S. all owe a debt for our stories' existence; for in fact, those of us with non-Native heritage were immigrants to their ancestral land and they have paid dearly for our poor treatment of them upon our ancestral arrival. For more history of the Native American plight under European immigrant conquests, see these books: Smith, *Conquest*; Zinn, *A People's History of The United States*.

19. For more on the history of African enslavement and the slave trade, see: Berlin, *Many Thousands Gone*; or again, as above: Zinn, *A People's History of The United States*.

immigrants allowed into the United States by using a national origins quota, meaning that the number of people allowed to enter the U.S. as immigrants would be limited to two percent of those people of the same nationality already living in the U.S. as of the 1890 census. The act also excluded all immigrants from Asia and gave priority to immigrants from white, European nations like those of British ancestry.[20] Following World War II, the country again revisited its immigration laws, instituting the Immigration and Nationality Act of 1952. This act ended Asian exclusion and introduced a system of preferences. These preference categories prioritized certain immigrants over others based on their special skills or close family ties (a system still used, with modifications, today). But the law, instituted in the midst of the Cold War, was still guided by national security concerns over Communist infiltration. While the world was getting smaller through the use of technology and communications, legislators debating the issue of immigration were seeking to separate from the global shifts to preserve national identity and become more isolationist out of fear of another form of government stripping away the (relatively recently understood) "American way of life."[21]

With the new and growing global population, the quota system of past immigration laws quickly became outdated and unsustainable. In 1965, the Immigration and Naturalization Act (Hart-Cellar Act) was passed by Congress, eliminating the quotas based on national origin and establishing a policy of immigration predominantly based on family reunification and the importing of skilled labor into the country. This act, still in place (though with many modifications over the years), was born of the civil rights movement, which saw the earlier quota systems as discriminatory. Then-president John F. Kennedy described the older system as "intolerable."[22] After the assassination of the president, Congress,

20. U.S. Department of State Office of the Historian, "The Immigration Act of 1924."

21. U.S. Department of State Office of the Historian, "The Immigration and Nationality Act of 1952."

22. "U.S. Immigration Since 1965," *History.*

including the late president's brother Ted Kennedy, heavily supported the new law. Congress and the new president, Lyndon B. Johnson, did not think the new law to be any kind of major revolution the way other civil rights laws had been, however. The move to include people from different countries was not meant to be a boon to immigration, but simply a less racially-partial system. But the bill's new and improved preference categories, including those for relatives of U.S. citizens and permanent residents, those with special work skills, and those from war-torn countries opened new doors for previously quota-capped countries to apply for residence in the U.S. Though still lined with per-country caps in some areas and caps on total immigration, the work of family reunification and the open doors to more Asian countries (including those fighting in Southeast Asia) and to more Eastern European countries faced with brutal communist regimes led to a threefold increase in immigration to the United States in the following three decades, as compared to the three decades preceding the law. In the 1950s, more than half of the nation's immigrants were European, only 6% Asian, and by the 1990s only 16% were European and 31% were Asian, and the Latino population expanded exponentially, with over 4.3 million immigrants from Mexico alone between 1965 and 2000.

The 1980s and 1990s conversation on immigration moved toward the issue of undocumented immigration, leading to a series of reforms to try to curtail the problems faced by employers, U.S. workers, and social welfare programs. While some bills provided some modicum of openness to immigrants who had entered the country illegally, others sought mainly to enforce border protection measures and detain and remove those who had entered the country without being properly vetted. With the growing public awareness of undocumented workers arriving from Mexico in the 1970s, a bill was passed in 1986 called the Immigration Reform and Control Act (IRCA), which primarily dealt with the issue of undocumented immigration. This bill provided amnesty for certain undocumented persons who had been present since 1982 (or who had worked on farms for several seasons during that time), allowing them to seek temporary, and then permanent residence. A second main feature of the IRCA was the "employer sanctions." This provision made it illegal for employers to knowingly hire undocumented workers. Both amnesty and employer sanctions provided legal avenues for immigrants to avoid being treated unfairly under the law, but amnesty did not provide new and better avenues for future immigrants. The employer sanctions made employers liable to enforce immigration laws, which some still continue to ignore, continuing to hire undocumented workers and exploiting them for cheap labor.[23]

In 1996 another major response to illegal immigration was passed called the Illegal Immigration Reform and Immigrant Responsibility Act (IIRAIRA), which addressed border enforcement and the use of social services by immigrants. More border patrol agents were deployed, new border control measures were implemented, government benefits were reduced for immigrants, avenues of relief and defense from deportation were limited, and the government introduced as a pilot program the "employment verification program," a voluntary electronic program whereby employers and social service agencies can attempt to verify the identity and eligibility of a worker or immigrant applying for public service benefits. Additionally, the law expanded the meaning of "aggravated felony" to include non-violent offenses that an immigrant may have been involved in before gaining immigration status. This retroactive new law required these immigrants to undergo mandatory detention, as they were suddenly defined as "aggravated felons." This same law established three-and ten-year bars on re-entry for any immigrant present in the United States without status, leading to a number of immigrants suddenly becoming fearful about leaving, as the bar would go up and they would be stranded outside the U.S. for up to a decade before they could then legally enter again. The circular migration of immigrants was effectively stopped with this legislation. The 1996 law also began the first strain of antiterrorism laws that "expedited procedures for the removal of suspected foreign terrorists from the United States,

23. Wilbanks, *Re-Creating America*.

allowed the detention and deportation of non-U.S. citizens on the basis of 'secret evidence' that neither they nor their attorneys are allowed to see, and instituted more stringent procedures for the granting of asylum."[24]

After the terrorist attacks of September 11, 2001, Congress passed the Homeland Security Act of 2002, which moved the former INS into the newly created the U.S. Department of Homeland Security (DHS).[25] In addition, "the federal government instituted a number of law-enforcement measures that targeted people of particular nationalities in the name of national security. Most infamously, a 'special registration' system (NSEERS) and a 'voluntary interview' program were instituted in 2002 that singled out foreign-born Muslims, Arabs, and South Asians,"[26] sadly a program making the news again, as the new administration decides about how to implement campaign promises to register potential terrorists (i.e., most Muslim and Arab immigrants), with little to no oversight to ensure the religious freedom and human rights of those Muslim and Arab immigrants in the U.S. with no ties to terrorism.[27] Also, several new laws that combine anti-terrorism concerns with renewed attempts to control undocumented immigration were passed:

> The Enhanced Border Security and Visa Entry Reform Act of 2002 implemented new procedures for the review of visa applicants and required that travel and entry documents be machine-readable, tamper-resistant, and include biometric identifiers. The REAL ID Act of 2005 required states to demand proof of citizenship or legal immigration status before issuing a driver's license, and to make driver's licenses resistant to fraud or tampering. The Secure Fence Act of 2006 called for the building of

24. Ewing, "Opportunity and Exclusion."

25. Congress of the United States, "Immigration Policy in the United States."

26. Ewing, "Opportunity and Exclusion."

27. Price and Patel, "Muslim Registry or NSEERS Reboot Would Be Unconstitutional."

an additional 850 miles of fencing along the U.S.-Mexico border.[28]

Reactions to these immigration laws have been intense. *Time* has reported that the border fencing and increased patrol of normal crossing areas are funneling the undocumented into remote deserts, leading to the deaths of many more immigrants than in previous years, while proponents say the fence and extra border control is working, keeping more people out of the country each day.[29] Since 2006, Congress has been debating various immigration bills, with many members of Congress wanting full-scale reform of what they see as a broken immigration system. Even as some of the more conservative members of Congress dismissed the bills as amnesty measures and the more liberal members would not pass them without more open-border and family reunification provisions, President George W. Bush pushed unsuccessfully for a decision from both parties.[30] Some bills have been proposed for comprehensive immigration reform in recent years, though none have bi-partisan support.[31] One of the bills, called the DREAM act,[32] so named as an acronym for "Development, Relief, and Education for Alien Minors," was first introduced in Congress in 2001 with bipartisan support,[33] but failed to become law, and even after having as many as 48 Congresspersons' support over the years (it was re-introduced multiple times between 2004–2009), with various votes on the measure, the act has never moved toward becoming law. This act would have allowed those undocumented college-bound high school students and current college students in the U.S. who were brought to the country by their parents as minor children to have a path for work and long-term residence. These students often have little to no connection to their country

28. Ewing, "Opportunity and Exclusion."

29. von Drehle, "The Great Wall of America."

30. Runtenberg, "Bush Takes On Conservatives Over Immigration."

31. Immigration Policy Center, "The Comprehensive Immigration Reform Act of 2010."

32. "The DREAM Act," *White House.*

33. American Immigration Council, "The DREAM Act."

of birth, and some may not even know they are in the country illegally until it is time to go to college. While some states have allowed for undocumented students to attend colleges at in-state tuition rates, others strictly prohibit state funds covering tuition for undocumented students. Despite how a student may excel in school in the only country they have ever known, many will never be able to find a pathway to residence and citizenship under current immigration law.

Because of the congressional deadlock on the issue of immigration, President Obama used executive authority in recent years to try to bridge the gap of immigration reform. June 2012 saw the first of a series of executive actions by the Obama administration to attempt to end-run congressional deadlock on pressing immigration issues. The president announced the government would accept requests for Deferred Action for Childhood Arrivals (DACA), a move designed to temporarily suspend the deportation of undocumented young people residing here who were brought to the United States as children by their undocumented parents.[34] These young people must meet criteria established under legislative proposals like the DREAM act, including if they:

1. Were under the age of 31 as of June 15, 2012;

2. Came to the United States before reaching their 16th birthday;

3. Have continuously resided in the United States since June 15, 2007, up to the present time;

4. Were physically present in the United States on June 15, 2012, and at the time of making their request for consideration of deferred action with USCIS;

5. Had no lawful status on June 15, 2012;

6. Are currently in school, have graduated or obtained a certificate of completion from high school, have obtained a general education development (GED) certificate, or are an

---

34. American Immigration Council, "Deferred Action for Childhood Arrivals."

honorably discharged veteran of the Coast Guard or Armed Forces of the United States; and

7. Have not been convicted of a felony, significant misdemeanor, or three or more other misdemeanors, and do not otherwise pose a threat to national security or public safety.[35]

In November 2014, President Obama announced his "Immigration Accountability Executive Action" that included a series of actions to provide new temporary immigration protections for many undocumented parents of U.S. citizens and lawful permanent residents, as well as "highly technical regulatory proposals to fix outdated visa provisions."[36] The main action in the reform is an expansion of DACA to include Deferred Action for Parents of Americans and Lawful Permanent Residents (DAPA) to provide temporary relief from deportation for parents of U.S. citizens (children born in the United States) as well as those with children who have gained lawful permanent residence (green cards). While the executive actions stem from the executive branch's authority to "exercise discretion in the prosecution and enforcement of immigration cases,"[37] allowing up to three years of deferred deportation of these classes of undocumented immigrants, the moves do not create paths to residence or citizenship, as this falls outside the scope of the executive branch's authority. Still, those who oppose any move to provide relief to these and other undocumented groups have forced much of the 2014 order into temporary injunction by the courts, with a Supreme Court review underway.[38]

Even with the former president's actions seeking some relief for some groups of undocumented immigrants, legal paths to residence and citizenship have not been approved by Congress and the long-term status of these individuals remains unknown,

35. United States Citizenship and Immigration Services (USCIS), "Consideration of Deferred Action for Childhood Arrivals (DACA)."

36. Immigration Policy Center, "A Guide to the Immigration Accountability Executive Action."

37. American Immigration Council, "Understanding the Legal Challenges to Executive Action."

38. Ibid.

leaving them less fearful in the immediate future, but still without long-term recourse to live in the United States permanently. And, President Obama, though largely immigrant-sympathetic, has fallen under great scrutiny for his administration's handling of immigrant deportation and detention over his two terms as president. Just three years into his presidency, in October 2011, PBS ran a documentary entitled "Lost in Detention," outlining the Obama administration's record-setting deportation and detention levels, including complaints of abuse.[39] Nearly two years later, in August 2013, complaints continued when the administration brought back the use of and expanded immigration family detention centers and raids by Immigration & Customs officials that separate families or lock up U.S. citizen children in detention with their undocumented parents. The process for deportation has been sped up, with largely disastrous results for families, as the bureaucratic processes can be fraught with errors and leave families with no legal representation or recourse to fight the deportation orders.[40]

The overall pattern of laws (excepting executive reprieves from deportation) have increasingly tightened U.S. borders and yet have never effectively dealt with undocumented immigrants living in the United States, nor deterred much the entrance of those without documentation. As we enter the second decade of the twenty-first century, the United States remains as collectively conflicted as ever when it comes to the issue of undocumented immigration. Recently, to attempt to deal with the immigration dilemma, some more conservative state governors and legislatures have begun tightening state laws affecting immigrants and seeking to use state power to usurp federal immigration law. States have taken various measures to change (largely restrict) the laws concerning undocumented immigrants. These laws have restricted undocumented immigrants seeking driver's licenses or in-state tuition at state universities and colleges, but others have gone even

39. "Lost in Detention," *PBS Frontline.*

40. Tan, "President Obama Wants to Continue Imprisoning Immigrant Families."

further.[41] For example, Arizona passed a state law SB 1070[42] that "includes provisions adding state penalties relating to immigration law enforcement including trespassing, harboring and transporting illegal immigrants, alien registration documents, employer sanctions, and human smuggling." The United States public is concerned for many reasons about the presence and activities of the undocumented population. Without federal immigration reform (more open or less open), states will continue the trend of attempting to preempt federal law with measures designed to restrict benefits of functioning in the state as an undocumented immigrant (dubbed "enforcement through attrition").

Even laws once regarded favorably on both sides of the political spectrum such as refugee and asylum cases are largely being attacked politically by states and politicians seeking to play on the fears of voters. Shortly after the Islamic State (ISIS) attacked civilians in Paris in November 2015, with the attacker pretending to be a Syrian refugee by carrying a Syrian passport, more than half (31) of U.S. state governors had declared they would not accept Syrian refugees for resettlement. Despite their politically and fear-driven announcements, however, state governments have no jurisdiction over federal immigration laws, including undocumented

---

41. For more information on state immigration laws, see National Conference of State Legislatures, "Immigration Policy Project."

42. "In April 2010, Arizona enacted two laws addressing immigration, SB 1070 and HB 2162. These laws added new state requirements, and created crimes and penalties related to enforcement of immigration laws and were to become effective on July 29, 2010. Before the laws could go into effect, the U.S. Department of Justice filed a lawsuit asking for an injunction against these laws arguing that they are unconstitutional. On July 28, Judge Bolton granted the request for injunction in part and enjoined those provisions related to state law officers determining immigration status during any lawful stop; the requirement to carry alien registration documents; the prohibition on applying for work if unauthorized; and permission for warrantless arrests if there is probable cause the offense would make the person is removable from the United States. Arizona Governor Jan Brewer has appealed the injunction and arguments will be heard by the 9th U.S. Circuit Court of appeals on Nov. 1, 2010." See: National Conference of State Legislatures, "Analysis of Arizona's Immigration Law."

immigration or refugee resettlement.[43] Even rather conservative judges, like David Godbey of the District Court of Austin, have ruled against the states seeking to sue the Obama administration regarding resettlement of refugees.[44]

Since the beginning of the Trump administration, multiple executive orders have been issued related to immigration. The first, and most provocative, was an order issued on January 25, 2017, just a week into his presidency, called "Executive Order: Border Security and Immigration Enforcement Improvements"[45] that barred any foreign national from seven majority-Muslim countries (Iraq, Syria, Iran, Libya, Somalia, Sudan and Yemen) from entering the US for 90 days, all refugees for 120 days, and any Syrian refugees indefinitely. The ensuing confusion from the order, including immigrants from these countries on flights bound for the U.S. being suddenly detained at the border, some of whom already held green cards, along with refugees nearing the completion of the vetting process suddenly having their plans derailed, left Customs and Border Patrol seeking further guidance, and lawyers fervently defending clients from the order, taking the case to the highest courts. A new executive order is in process at the time of this writing that will likely address some of the confusing issues for the border patrol officers and Department of Homeland Security, but will not backtrack much on the restricting of immigration from the same Muslim-majority countries.[46] Executive orders, once criticized by the far right, are now the vehicle by which the country's top leader has chosen to drive the immigration policy further to toward mass deportation of low-income workers with U.S. family members, fewer visa options for all categories, and an unwelcoming U.S. presence in the world.

The ever-tightening borders, as well as laws and statements seeking to deter further immigration or even force out undocumented immigrants (and perhaps all immigrants, or at least

---

43. Gulasekaram and Ramakirshnan, "The Law is Clear."

44. "Texas," *The New York Times.*

45. "Executive Order," White House Press Office.

46. de Vogue and Kopan, "New Trump travel ban order nearing completion."

immigrants of certain countries or ethnicities or faiths), have left United States immigration policy at a crossroads. Either the country will work toward immigrant-positive rhetoric and laws or continue to tighten laws and force out whole groups of people (either by removing their voice from the national conversation on immigration or removing their person or their family members through deportation). Sadly, no group of immigrants is immune to what largely amounts to racism and xenophobia on the part of some vocal groups of people in power, and undocumented immigrants bear the brunt of most of the struggle. They are largely poor and uneducated, seeking a new life and education in the United States, and the process for finding ways to live permanently here are at best confusing and at worst, completely out of reach.

Immigration: The Process

Even when new immigrants want to follow the law, the complexities of the systems involved for immigration make the process difficult. In order to immigrate permanently to the United States, for the most part, an individual must be sponsored by either an employer or qualifying family member, be randomly selected from countries who do not send many immigrants through sponsorship paths (called the Diversity Visa Lottery Program), or show fear of persecution in one's home country on account of immutable characteristics (asylum and refugee status). To obtain status, the parties involved must complete a series of forms and processes and prove financial support. The costs for these processes can be substantial, as the government filing fees alone for just one step in the process can be over $1,000 per person. Many immigrants need help filing their documents, which adds on attorney fees or requires help from a local charitable organization. Employer sponsorship often involves processes to show unavailability of U.S. workers. Numbers of visas in each category are limited and issued on an annual basis with arbitrary visa number caps. Waits for visa numbers can take years, even decades, for some lower-skilled workers or family members of permanent residents or siblings of U.S. citizen sponsors. The process is simpler and the line shorter, however, for the higher-skilled laborers, executives, and close family members, such as spouses and children of U.S. citizen sponsors (excepting those who happen to have sneaked across the border more than once, as a legal bar would prevent them from re-entering the U.S. for three or ten years, or perhaps even permanently).

Once immigrants obtain permanent status, they receive a permanent resident card, more commonly known as a green card,[47] that allows them to live and work in the United States permanently. Nevertheless, even a permanent resident can have their status revoked or even be deported for such offenses as claiming to be a U.S. citizen, voting, staying abroad for too long a period of time, or committing certain crimes. Permanent residents in good standing can in turn sponsor other qualifying family members for residence as well, though for nationals of certain countries (like Mexico, China, and India), this sponsorship path can take years, even decades. After holding a green card for five years, permanent residents can apply for naturalization by submitting a lengthy biographical questionnaire, undergoing biometrically-based criminal record checks, and passing an English and U.S. history/civics examination. The current government fee for this process is $725, plus any private fees to cover help with learning English or understanding U.S. civics.

Breaking Down the Current Problems with the System

The Immigration Policy Center (IPC) issued a detailed and helpful report entitled "Breaking Down the Problems: What's Wrong With

---

47. The "green card" is a common name for the (until recently, pinkish-white) card, form I-551. The card contains a photo of the immigrant, details the immigrant's name, date of birth, alien registration number ("A" number), date of admission as a permanent resident, and expiration date of the document itself (as the status does not expire). As of May 2010, these permanent residence cards are green once again, with further security measures in place to protect against fraud (see USCIS, "New Design: The Green Card Goes Green," for further information on these changes).

Our Immigration System" in October 2009, which I will lean on heavily as a relevant source of information on the pitfalls of our current immigration system. IPC was created as a research body, part of the American Immigration Council, which seeks "to shape rational conversation on immigration on and immigrant integration . . . Formed in 2003, [IPC is] a non-partisan organization that neither supports nor opposes any political party or candidate . . . [IPC's] work helps to bridge the gap between advocates and academics, policy experts and politicians. Through forums, briefings, and special publications, [IPC brings] diverse groups together to help shape the immigration debate."[48] With this in mind, their thoughtful analysis of the immigration dilemma in the United States is unparalleled and immigrant-friendly, which as noted in later chapters, is a Christian ideal. In its publication, IPC notes that the problems with immigration in the United States do not center solely on the problem of having 11 million undocumented immigrants, but instead involve a broader range of issues, including structural failure of the current immigration system and inadequate responses on the part of the federal government to address these issues. The general information contained in this report will be summarized here.[49] There are other organizations who take differing stances toward these problems and how to solve them;[50] however, because the Immigration Policy Center focuses its energies on protecting families and supporting immigrants (biblical goals, as explored in later chapters), this study will primarily focus on these issues and strategies.

The IPC report begins by highlighting five areas of the immigration system "that are broken and need remedy."[51] First, family-based immigration has backlogs that keep families sepa-

---

48. Immigration Policy Center, "Mission."

49. Immigration Policy Center, "Breaking Down the Problems."

50. See the Center for Immigration Studies (CIS) for competing views that focus on deportation/removal of most, if not all, immigrants in the United States, along with enhanced border control and stricter immigration laws, *Center for Immigration Studies*, online: http://www.cis.org/

51. Immigration Policy Center, "Breaking Down the Problems," 7.

rated. There are three main causes for this: (1) "Demand exceeds supply": U.S. citizens can apply for visas for their immediate family (spouses, children, and parents) without regard to number caps, but other family members such as children over the age of twenty-one must wait years. In addition, those immigrants who only hold a green card must wait even longer to sponsor family members; (2) "Per-country limits create long backlogs in certain countries": A 1976 law created per-country caps for all countries, meaning Mexico has the same numbers available as all other even with a higher number of immigrants in demand from that country—specifically, 7% of the total in any category. That means countries that have higher immigration rates to the U.S. (Mexico, China, the Philippines) must wait much longer for visas than those from other countries; (3) "Processing delays and inconsistent policies heighten problems and create more illegal entry": Lack of resources and rigid bureaucratic procedures have not allowed the immigration system to work expeditiously to conduct quick background checks or coordinate visas between agencies (the DHS and the Department of State). While waiting for a green card, family members have almost no chance of getting a temporary visa to travel to visit the U.S., leaving families apart for the many years it takes to procure one.[52]

Second, the "employment-based visa system is not responsive to employers' labor needs." Only 140,000 employment-based green cards are available annually to qualified immigrants. This arbitrary number was chosen by Congress many years ago without regard to real labor-market needs and "has not been updated to conform to current economic realities."[53] The ebb and flow of need in an economy would require consistent monitoring to know how many visas should be issued each year. For example, in a recession, the 140,000 may be sufficient, but when the economy turns around, U.S. employers will need more workers. Some will only need temporary workers, but others will require permanent workers for their positions and may not be able to procure a permanent

52. Ibid.
53. Ibid., 8.

visa under that year's allocated numbers (or any upcoming years, as they allow the worker to remain in temporary work visa status waiting on a permanent number). As such, the current system cannot meet the ever-changing economic needs of the United States. Additionally, there are only 5,000 permanent residence visas allocated annually for less-skilled workers, such as hotel workers, landscapers, and construction workers. IPC believes the insufficient number of green cards for these workers is at the heart of the unauthorized immigration issue. The industries that need these workers cannot meet their demands with local labor pools and petitioning for workers is backlogged for many, many years. IPC states, "until there are more legal avenues for employers to hire immigrant workers to meet economic demands, unauthorized immigration will continue to fill the gap, and we will not be able to regain control over immigration."[54]

Third, "millions of unauthorized workers and other immigrants, many with U.S.-citizen families, reside in the United States with no means to become legal residents."[55] The laws and regulations that penalize behaviors such as overstaying a visa or working without authorization "often produce unintended and illogical results."[56] Many of these minor infractions carry extreme consequences with few exceptions for waivers. For example, as mentioned previously, the IIRIRA of 1996 "created bars on admission to the United States for individuals who have been unlawfully present in the country."[57] These bars state that persons who have been unlawfully present in the United States for more than 180 days but less than one year and who voluntarily depart may not enter the country again for three years. People unlawfully present for more than one year are subject to a ten-year bar on re-entry. Because of such laws, people otherwise qualified for work or family visas are unable to adjust their status, and if they leave the country to get a visa at a consulate abroad, they cannot re-enter the

54. Ibid.
55. Ibid.
56. Ibid.
57. Ibid.

United States until the time of the bar has elapsed. Thus, unauthorized immigrants who are eligible for visas often are encouraged by these laws to remain in the country without status rather than risk separation from their families for three or ten years (or possibly permanently).[58]

Fourth, "unscrupulous employers who hire unauthorized workers in order to maximize profits are lowering wages and working conditions for ALL workers."[59] Without status, unauthorized workers are vulnerable to abuse by unscrupulous employers because they cannot organize to petition against poor working conditions or low wages for fear of deportation. And, those employers trying to follow the law are competitively at a disadvantage because they choose not to use low-wage labor to enhance their bottom lines.[60]

Fifth and lastly, "inadequate infrastructure causes delays in the integration of immigrants who want to become U.S. citizens."[61] Integration (learning English, understanding and adapting to U.S. culture, etc.) is an important aspect of immigration for most Americans because it enables immigrants to contribute to the country and realize their full potential. The United States, however, has no comprehensive integration strategy. Immigrants have little access to ESL programs as funding continually gets cut for these programs, despite higher demands. And, as stated previously, the naturalization process is costly and demanding.[62]

The report goes on to discuss the inadequate government responses to these issues. Even when the federal government has been spending billions of dollars on border enforcement, the number of undocumented immigrants in the United States has nearly tripled since 1990. In addition, 25–40% of all unauthorized immigrants do not sneak across the border but instead enter legally and overstay their visas. Since 1992, the annual budget

58. Ibid., 9.
59. Ibid.
60. Ibid.
61. Ibid., 10.
62. Ibid.

of the U.S. Border Patrol has increased by 714 percent and the number of Border Patrol agents along the southwest border has grown 390 percent.[63] But "border security without adequate legal channels for immigration has created a more dangerous border and reduced 'circularity' of migration."[64] The enhanced border security at traditional points of entry has diverted immigrants to more dangerous areas, and the probability of death or injury has increased dramatically, up to one per day. Because of this danger, many immigrants cannot survive the journey alone and hire a smuggler, most of whom charge thousands for their services. The debt owed the smuggler often ends up following the immigrant for months or years and can endanger the lives of the immigrant's family members. Once here, the immigrants are very likely to stay because of the enhanced security measures. Before such measures were in place, many immigrants were 'circular' meaning that they would come for short periods to work and then return to their home countries in a repeating pattern.[65]

The report then notes that this "enforcement culture" created by the enforcement measures is actively criminalizing immigration violations and resulting in mistakes by law enforcement in the violation of immigrants' civil rights. Because of the focus on identifying and detaining unauthorized immigrants for deportation, the government has expanded its priorities to include the ever-expanding Immigration and Customs Enforcement (ICE) detention system. "ICE operates the largest detention and supervised-release program in the country. A total of 378,582 immigrants from 221 countries were in custody or supervised by ICE in FY 2008."[66] The crimes for which immigrants may be deported and the crimes for which immigrants get mandatory detention have expanded, and the budget for ICE has nearly doubled between 2005 and 2009. The report notes that many unauthorized immigrants live in mixed-status communities (some family members and neighbors

63. Ibid., 13.
64. Ibid., 14.
65. Ibid., 15.
66. Ibid., 16.

are U.S. citizens and Lawful Permanent Residents). When ICE raids workplaces and performs door-to-door raids, these family members and neighbors are directly affected, especially the U.S.-citizen children who are left in an untenable situation when one or both parents are deported. Moreover, this enforcement has led to numerous mistakes and violations of civil rights; even U.S. citizens have been erroneously detained and deported.[67]

The report then states that "the enforcement-only model has pushed immigrants further underground, undermining community safety and national security."[68] Undocumented immigrants are less likely to report crimes or cooperate with authorities in criminal investigations for fear of deportation, making everyone in a community less safe. Sometimes ICE works directly with local police to find and detain undocumented immigrants, frightening the immigrant population and slowing the criminal processing for other, violent crimes. Furthermore, the enforcement-only method is not enhancing national security. By spending billions identifying undocumented immigrants and creating a border situation where smugglers and traffickers decide who makes it into the country, the American public cannot feel secure. The government needs to bring these undocumented individuals out of the shadows by correctly identifying them and encourage people to enter the country through legal channels. This in turn would allow law-enforcement and border-enforcement agents to focus on people who pose a threat to public safety or national security.[69]

In closing, the report notes that:

> It is clear that relentlessly building up enforcement resources has not worked in the past and is not a realistic solution to our current problems. The underlying flaws of the legal immigration system must be addressed first. The United States must create a fair, humane, and practical immigration system for the 21st century that is

67. Ibid.
68. Ibid., 17.
69. Ibid.

responsive to the needs of our economy and encourages legal behavior.[70]

Economic and Social Fears

According to Dana W. Wilbanks in his book *Re-Creating America*, the most influential view about why immigrants come to the United States is the "push-pull" theory. The "push factors" in the home country are circumstances that make individuals want to leave the country. The "pull factors" from within the United States are ways in which the United States lures migrants, which can include tangible necessities, such as better jobs and wages, or intangible desires, such as better general opportunities. Wilbanks also states that other forces may be at work besides simple push-pull factors, such as the dynamics of the global economic systems which move labor across borders, as well as established trade of labor between neighboring countries.[71]

Despite the reasons these undocumented immigrants come, many Americans still struggle with how their presence is affecting the U.S. economy, public welfare, and taxes. Many assume that undocumented immigrants are draining the U.S. economy and costing billions to maintain, largely due to the voices of nativist commentators like Bill O'Reilly's "Talking Points"[72] and more militant immigration opponent groups such as the Minutemen Project. This latter group, based in California, waxes and wanes as the group leaders often face prison time for their efforts. Their goals are the immediate forced removal of all "illegals" as well as stricter border enforcement (often resorting to their own patrol of the border). They say that the government cannot or will not handle the issue of undocumented immigration, and thus their volunteers must take up arms to patrol the 2,000 mile border with

70. Ibid., 18.

71. Wilbanks, *Re-Creating America*, 68.

72. An example of the rhetoric used by Bill O'Reilly and others on Fox News can be found at: "The Left's Secret Immigration Plan," *Fox News*.

Mexico (which they did from 2005–2010). The movement died down some after one of its key members robbed and murdered a Border Patrol Agent in 2010, but one of their leaders, John Gilchrest, has continued to be vocal about issues related to immigration, accusing the Obama administration of not taking the "threat" of undocumented immigration seriously enough (despite the administration's influx of over 21,000 more border patrol agents), periodically vowing to reinstate civilian border patrols.[73] Still other groups, such as the Center for Immigration Studies (CIS), which was named to sound like an immigration-neutral think tank, are in fact distributing anti-immigrant propaganda, systematically working to increase restrictions on foreigners and to limit immigration reform. CIS is closely allied with the Federation for American Immigration Reform (FAIR),[74] a group that provides "facts" concerning foreigners and aims to demonize their presence in the United States.[75]

When the numbers are evaluated, however, the picture changes. For example, the 1986 immigration law made employers legally liable for hiring undocumented immigrants, so many undocumented immigrants have since resorted to using fake IDs, including fake social security numbers, to gain employment. Employers thus have hired the workers under the impression that the worker had legal status. When the Social Security Administration

73. Miller, "Minuteman Project Ready to Return to Border Amid Wave of Illegal Immigration."

74. Federation for American Immigration Reform (FAIR) is a self-proclaimed, "non-profit, non-partisan organization of concerned individuals who believe that our immigration laws must be reformed to better serve the needs of current and future generations . . . FAIR seeks to reduce overall immigration to a level that is more manageable and which more closely reflects past policy. Reducing legal immigration from well over one million presently, to 300,000 a year over a sustained period will allow America to more sensibly manage its growth, address its environmental needs, and maintain a high quality of life . . . America has reached a point where perpetual growth cannot realistically continue within limited space. FAIR believes that without common sense limitations on immigration and the resulting population growth, virtually every social cause is a lost cause."

75. Hake, "What the Bible Really Says about Immigration Policy."

(SSA) began to see in the 1980s that these numbers were not matching the bearer's name (or were simply fake), they held off fully investigating the matter and began receiving a surplus of money from these "no match" social security numbers.[76] Over $189 billion worth of wages was recorded in this SSA fund in the 1990s. The file is now growing, on average, "by more than $50 billion a year, generating $6 billion to $7 billion in Social Security tax revenue and about $1.5 billion in Medicare taxes."[77] While the SSA cannot definitively say that all of the money from the "no match" numbers is from undocumented immigrants, they suspect a large percentage is. The SSA's chief actuary says that the administration thinks that about three-fourths of undocumented immigrants pay payroll taxes using false or fake social security numbers.[78] In addition to payroll taxes, all undocumented immigrants also pay sales tax when they shop and pay property taxes (either directly as homeowners or as part of their monthly rent payment), consistently adding to the U.S. economy's growth.[79]

Undocumented immigrants may actually help with the deficit of money in government agencies because they are ineligible for most government benefits. Undocumented immigrants cannot legally obtain Temporary Aid for Needy Family (TANF), or welfare, cannot collect food stamps or live in public housing, have no disability benefits, and cannot get Medicare or Medicaid. In some states, the only public aid an undocumented immigrant *might* be eligible for is "emergency and prenatal healthcare, immunizations

76. The SSA began sending "no match" letters to employers in 1994 when a social security number produced a "no match." Largely employers ignored these violations. In September 2007, the Department of Homeland Security proposed its safe harbor rule that required the SSA to insert a letter from ICE with the "no match" letter to the employer. This letter warned the employer not to ignore the "no match" designations because they could be fined heavily. President Obama has now pulled that rule and the SSA has not resumed sending "no match" letters. See this explanatory article for more detail on the history of "no match" letters and the SSA: Migration Policy Institute, "Social Security 'No-Match' Letters: A Primer."

77. Porter, "Illegal Immigrants Are Bolstering Social Security With Billions."

78. Ibid.

79. Soerens and Hwang, *Welcoming the Stranger*, 34–35.

and treatment for communicable diseases, certain nutritional programs aimed primarily at children, and noncash emergency disaster relief (such as in the wake of Hurricane Katrina)."[80] Children of undocumented immigrants may attend school as well, but no undocumented immigrant can legally receive any cash benefit from the government. Even many documented immigrants are ineligible for public benefits. Immigrants need to have been permanent residents for at least five years before they can receive any welfare funds for their family (with a few exceptions).[81] While it is true that many undocumented immigrants use stolen or fraudulent identities to gain employment, there is no way to calculate what government benefits, if any, they have obtained using those same identities. Unfortunately, the systems used by welfare agencies to check identity can only detect fake identities, not stolen ones. ICE is leading an investigation into identity theft by immigrants; however their efforts are not well funded due to more pressing concerns, such as drug smuggling and violent criminals.[82] Many immigrants use fraudulent and stolen identities mainly to seek employment, not maliciously.[83]

Once Christians have evaluated the legal and historical realities with a critical eye, there is yet more work to be done. Namely, Christians must not only think with their head about issues of moral importance, they must also explore their faith tradition through study of Scripture and the stories that make up the foundation of their worldview. In that process, too, they must begin the hard work of listening to the people who have been marginalized and used as political pawns in our ever-growing struggle against those considered "other."

---

80. Ibid., 42.

81. Ibid.

82. Immigration and Customs Enforcement, "ICE Investigations."

83. Leland, "Some ID Theft Is Not for Profit, but to Get a Job."

2

Telling the Stories, Part I

Stories are the "face" of facts, the human background of information that creates space for those who are marginalized and oppressed to speak and potentially to actually be heard by their oppressors and the privileged living among them. Oftentimes, stories are set aside as something less important than statistics or facts, when, from a Christian point of view, stories are the very foundation of faith. For Christians who take seriously the role of Scripture in their everyday lives, stories are inherently part of the tradition of response to ethical issues. The Bible has a myriad of stories regarding the understanding of the role of the stranger or foreigner as well as their treatment, and though these stories are often not told "from the margins" but to the established society of Israel, they raise up the marginalized to a place of prominence not often given to outsiders in ancient Near Eastern cultures, as will be examined in more detail in this chapter. Because of this, the work of interpretation from the margins (feminist, Black liberationist, Womanist, *Mujerista*) can see not only the work of God among the privileged Israelites but those who find themselves living and working among these tribes and this nation. The work of interpretation must also not preclude the troublesome texts, some of which seem quite xenophobic, but the trajectory of the Hebrew Bible and the work of Jesus in the New Testament overwhelmingly provide ample foundation for a Christian ethic of inclusion of the stranger.

Telling the Biblical Stories:
Old Testament Narrative and Law

Understanding what the Bible says to the issue of undocumented immigration necessarily must begin with a discussion of what it means in Scripture to be human and to be a migrant. Genesis 1 opens the discussion to the movement of *human beings* as immigrants. To be human is to be loved by God and made in the *imago dei* (image of God). Without first recognizing the humanity of the individuals involved, the tendency is to treat the "illegals" as less than human, not deserving of consideration.[1]

Following this grounding in human dignity, the Genesis narratives provide specific examples of God's special care for the "alien" or "sojourner" living outside his or her homeland.[2] The stories of the patriarchs and matriarchs are fraught with instances of kindness to strangers; oftentimes, they are strangers themselves in foreign lands. For example, Abram (later Abraham) begins his journey from his homeland of Ur as an immigrant to Haran and later to Canaan (Gen 11:31—12:9), but famine drove him to seek food in Egypt (Gen 12:10). When confronted with strangers in his own home, he serves as a model of hospitality, eagerly offering them food and drink and running out to greet them (Gen 18:1–6). Abraham knew the perils of being a stranger in a foreign land and made these strangers (messengers of God, unbeknownst to him) feel welcome.

Abraham's family continued the tradition of becoming the stranger in the persons of Isaac, who moved to Philistine land to escape famine (Gen 35:27), Jacob, who sojourned in a foreign land when running from his brother's wrath (Gen 28:4; 32:4), and Jacob's sons, who went to Egypt twice for food during a famine (Gen 47:4, 9). For example, Joseph, who was sold into Egypt, faced many challenges as an alien, being blamed for someone else's

---

1. Groody, "Crossing the Divide," 4.

2. This Old Testament and Hebrew word study will rely foundationally, though not entirely, on the study conducted by Carroll R. in his book, *Christians at the Border*, 63–112.

misconduct (Gen 39) and then finding through inspired events a refuge with the Pharaoh himself (Gen 41:41). Joseph's influence in Egypt protected his family for many generations (Gen 41–50). When this protection ended, however, the nation of Israel was forced into slavery by the Egyptians (Exod 1). This story of the Hebrews' sojourn in Egypt "provides a cardinal example of the potential for tyranny and oppression on the part of a community or people over strangers and aliens who reside in their midst." [3] This was because the Egyptian Pharaoh feared the population of Hebrews was growing too rapidly, and his subsequent restriction of the population (Exod 1:16) led to God's conflict with the Pharaoh and the miraculous freeing of the Hebrews from his control. Other Old Testament works such as Psalms and Second Isaiah remember Israel as sojourners in Egypt (Ps 105:23; Isa 52:4) and God's deliverance is remembered in how the Israelites were expected to treat the strangers in their midst. [4]

Some figures in the Old Testament traveled *into* Israel as immigrants, such as Ruth, the immigrant from the land of Moab. She married a foreigner (an Israelite) while in her native land and even after his death chose to continue to live with her Israelite mother-in-law Naomi, migrating back to Judah with her. In this new land, Ruth became an immigrant in a society where the law was not favorable to Moabites (c.f. Num 22–25; Deut 23:3). Through perseverance and hard work gathering in the fields to provide for herself and her mother-in-law, this immigrant woman won the favor of Naomi's kinsman Boaz who redeemed Naomi's property and married Ruth. This marriage later resulted in the lineage of King David, and subsequently of Jesus. The Old Testament portrays many other immigrants, but not all can be discussed here; suffice it to say that the story of the immigrant is prevalent in the Old Testament narratives of heroism and struggle.

Four Hebrew words are used in the Old Testament to refer to foreigners: the nouns *gēr* and *tôšab* and the adjectives *nokrî* and

---

3. Miller, "Israel as Host to Strangers," 560.

4. Ibid.

zār.[5] Unfortunately, English translations of the Old Testament text are often inconsistent when rendering these terms. Sometimes the same English word is used for several of them, and sometimes different English words are used for the same Hebrew term. The last two words, *nokrî* and *zār*, describe someone or something that is non-Israelite. Sometimes this is neutral usage; for instance, Ruth tells Boaz she is a foreigner (*nokriyyâ*, Ruth 2:10). Other times, these terms can carry a negative connotation. They can be used to describe enemies (*zār*, Isa 1:7; 29:5), strange gods (*zār*, Deut 32:16; Jer 2:25), or foreign women who could corrupt Israel's men (*nokrî*, 1 Kgs 1:11). Still other times, *nokrî* (and sometimes *zār*) can refer to foreigners dwelling in Israel. The scant textual evidence available suggests either that the people have not been in the land very long (2 Sam 15:19) or that the people have not fully integrated into Israelite life (Deut 17:15; Isa 2:6; 1 Kings 8:41,43).[6]

The term *tôšab* only occurs a few times in the Old Testament and thus is hard to define. It is almost always found together with other nouns such as the Hebrew words for "hireling" or "sojourner."[7] This type of foreigner seems to be economically dependent on society and there seems to be a distinction between the *tôšab* and the *gēr* (sojourner) for them to be mentioned together. They also appear with the *nokrî* in the prohibitions about the Passover (Exod 12:43, 45), so it is possible that they too are not fully assimilated into the culture. But without much textual evidence, conclusions cannot be firmly drawn.[8]

The most pertinent term for the study of immigration is the word *gēr*. This word appears in much of the legal material of the Pentateuch and is translated in various English translations as "alien," "resident alien," "stranger," or "sojourner." The verb from which the noun derives (*gûr*) means "to dwell for a (definite or

---

5. Carroll R., 99.

6. Ibid.

7. With "hireling" Exod 12:45; Lev 22:10; 25:6, 40; with "sojourner" Lev 25:23, 35, 47; Num 35:15, Carroll R., 101.

8. Ibid., 101.

indefinite) time, dwell as a new-comer without rights."[9] The *gēr* was an outsider who entered the culture/nation of Israel to live for an indefinite time. The *gēr* might have come because of famine, searching for food, or because of military or other conflicts in their native land. The *gēr* would likely live in his or her new community permanently, or at least an extended period of time. For example, in 2 Sam 1:13, the Amalekite messenger who brings David the news of Saul's death describes himself as the son of sojourners. His family has thus been in Israel some time, as he had become a soldier in the Israelite militia. This might suggest a more appropriate modern term of "resident alien," [10] conveying both that the person was a stranger to the culture/nation of Israel and that the person now resides within Israel.[11] Additionally, the term might be used to describe an Israelite outside of his or her homeland. When Moses' son was born in Midian, he named him Gershom because "I have been a *gēr* in a foreign land" (Exod 2:22).[12]

Old Testament legal codes contrast sharply with the contemporary Ancient Near Eastern law codes on the issue of the sojourner. For instance, other law codes in existence in the ancient Near East (Assyria, Babylon, and Persia) offer little to no guidance concerning people emigrating from these nations. There are very few laws dealing with the rights of someone who leaves and returns (c.f. Laws of Eshnunna, law 30; Laws of Hammurabi, laws 30, 31, 136).[13] And even the one reference to a foreigner in Law 41 of the Laws of Eshnunna (possibly a merchant, though its inter-

9. Miller, 552.

10. Contrary to some interpretations, however, this term cannot be equated with a "permanent resident" as described in U.S. law. While the Old Testament offers guidance on how to treat foreigners, proper interpretation cannot simply be a one to one correspondence with modern laws and must be taken within its own context [c.f. Hoffmeier, *The Immigration Crisis*, for an example of a one to one interpretation].

11. Miller, 552.

12. Horner, "Changing Concepts of the 'Stranger' in the Old Testament," 50.

13. Pritchard, *Ancient Near Eastern Texts Relating to the Old Testament*, 161–98.

pretation is disputed) lacks any substance regarding the foreigner who came to live there, whatever the reason or circumstance. The Old Testament, on the other hand, offers numerous references not only to stories of strangers and immigrants, but cites them in laws and deals with different types of sojourners and foreigners directly. These laws are not just numerous; they are often gracious as well.[14]

The Old Testament has clear mandates for the love and mercy given to the immigrant. As stated, these laws were formulated to remind the nation of Israel of their history in Egypt, as oppressed aliens in a foreign land. God commanded them that given their experience, they should gladly welcome the stranger (immigrant) among them and not fear them, as the Egyptians had done to the Hebrews. The most memorable of these is Leviticus 19:33–34, which states, "When an alien resides with you in your land, you shall not oppress the alien. The alien who resides with you shall be to you as the citizen among you; you shall love the alien as yourself, for you were aliens in Egypt: I am the LORD your God."[15] The most common laws regarding the sojourner or alien are the gleaning laws. These laws provide for the sojourners and aliens in that the Israelites are "enjoined from picking up the remnants of the harvests of grain, olives, and grapes" (Lev 19:9–10; 23:22; Deut 24:19–21).[16] In addition, other laws, such as the tithing laws (Deut 14:28–29; 26:12), provided for the aliens' and sojourners' welfare. Israelites were to tithe to provide regular donations of food for those persons to eat.[17]

Because of the immigrant's vulnerability, God commands special care for them. Often, the Hebrew word for "alien" or "sojourner" is accompanied by the words for "orphan" and "widow" (e.g., Deut 10:18, 14:28–29, 16:11–14, 24:19–21, 26:12; Ps 146:9; Jer 22:3; Zech 7:10; Mal 3:5). Widows were entirely dependent on the (male-dominated) social structure because they had no rights, no physical strength. Orphans were often not of an age to be able

14. Carroll R., 102.

15. All Scripture citations are from the NRSV unless otherwise noted.

16. Miller, 562.

17. Ibid., 563.

to fend for themselves. Immigrants, too, were dependent on the society to which they had immigrated, having no family ties or inheritance to sustain them. In most cases, widows, orphans, and immigrants were poor and easily outcast, but the laws of God demanded specific care for them. The laws of the Torah were directed at those groups with the most precarious social positions—and the very delineation of words for different stages of immigrants suggests that Israel (like all cultures) saw them and treated them differently, and sometimes in a hostile way. The laws concerning the immigrant offered a specific answer to the question of "why should I?" noting that all Israelites should care for the outcast in society because it is a special concern for God (Ps 146:9; c.f. Deut 10:18).[18] The prophets continued to admonish the people of Israel, often strongly chiding them for their failure to care for these powerless. They claimed it was an infidelity to the LORD and that the LORD would not tolerate their disobedience (Jer 23:3; Ezek 22:7, 29; Mal 3:5; c.f. Ps 94:6).[19]

One of the most intimate ways Israel opened its heart to the sojourner was through allowing the sojourners to participate in its religion, its foundational identity as a people. Sojourners could participate "in the Sabbath, the Day of Atonement (Lev 16:29–30), the Passover (Exod 12:48–49; Num 9:14), the Feast of Weeks (Deut 16:11), the Feast of Tabernacles (Deut 16:14), and Firstfruits (Deut 26:11). Forgiveness for unintentional sin was extended to them (Num 15:27–29), and they were afforded access to the cities of refuge (Num 35:15)."[20] In addition, the sojourner's assimilation into the culture included some expectations and responsibilities. For example, they were to be present at the reading of the law (Deut 31:10–13) to learn how to be a member of the society. They were subject to "penalties of criminal laws (Lev 24:22), many dietary restrictions (Exod 12:19; Lev 17:10–15), the sexual taboos (Lev 18:26), purity laws (Num 19:10) . . . the prohibition against the worship of other gods and blasphemy against the LORD (Lev

---

18. Gowan, "Wealth and Poverty," 341–53.

19. Carroll R., 103.

20. Ibid., 105.

20:1–2; 24:10–16; Num 15:30–31)."[21] Still, the sojourners were distinct in that not all dietary laws applied (Deut 14:21).[22]

Though the majority of Old Testament texts unmistakably welcome the immigrant as neighbor to the children of Israel, some obvious tensions concerning Israel's relationship with foreign cultures are also present in the Scriptures. The rhetoric of Deuteronomy 7, in which the Deuteronomistic Historian poses a complete annihilation of various outside ethnic and religious groups (Canaanites, Amorites, Hittites, etc.) tends to shock modern readers who are not reading in context with the writing. The words are harsh and call for unmerciful destruction of nations, "utterly destroy[ing]" (Heb *herem*) them and avoiding all contact with their way of life. One scholar noted the following concerning *herem* ("utter destruction"):

1. The extreme force of the injunction to destroy is a negative counterpart to the first commandment 'only YHWH.' That is, because YHWH is a jealous God and will tolerate no rival, every such practitioner is subject to destruction as an act of obedience to the command of YHWH.

2. The threat of the other religious options is perceived not simply as political and cultural, but as *mythic*. That is, alternative religious practice has the potential to bring deep disorder into the community. The elimination of such a religious option therefore is to overcome the danger of *chaos* and so to assure the good order of society intended by YHWH as creator.

3. Because the seven nations are long gone, the rhetoric in this text is now to be understood *symbolically and not literally*; Israel has long since given up its readiness to undertake such barbaric actions.[23]

Whether or not Israelite readers saw the Deuteronomistic Historian's rhetoric as symbolic, the theme of keeping order in

21. Ibid., 106.

22. Ibid.

23. Brueggemann, *Deuteronomy*, 95.

community on a theological level is very clear. Association with rival religious and cultural groups had the potential to cause great social breakdown in post-exilic Israel (presumably when this book was composed, or at least edited into a whole). "The actual issue is that an alien presence and ideology, presumably the Assyrians, currently threaten Israel, and the danger of assimilation to foreign practices is very real."[24] This airtight social separation kept Israel from making a counter-covenant against YHWH through their covenant with these peoples.[25]

Deuteronomy 23 continues the theme of exclusion, despite many calls for care for sojourners in the land in the same book. The reluctance of the Deuteronomistic Historian to include other nationalities in temple worship continues the tradition of the post-exilic community "struggling with its identity and integrity."[26] The tradition of Ezra-Nehemiah drew on laws such as these to require Israel to put away foreign wives and children (again, a decision many modern readers abhor—e.g., Ezra 9–10; Neh 13). Ezra's words and actions were drenched in fear, as Israel fought to re-gain a foothold in their native land after many years of exile. The 'abominations' perpetrated by these people of the lands were likely issues of syncretism, which could have endangered the integrity of Israel's faith. Nehemiah continued this strand in Nehemiah 13, saying "the Ammonite and the Moabite should not come into the congregation forever." Nehemiah takes seriously the commands concerning foreign wives, speaking of the sins of Solomon, insisting again that strange wives should be sent away. Neither Ezra nor Nehemiah, however, deals with the issue of the *gēr* and the injunctions about kindness toward the *gēr*. Jewish scholar Hyam Maccoby notes that

> The danger of oppression of the *gēr* occurred only in a settled Israelite community, where a population of *gērîm* arose through influx from outside countries, attracted by economic or religious motives. The community of

24. Nelson, *Deuteronomy*, 99.

25. Ibid.

26. Brueggeman, 229.

Ezra-Nehemiah . . . did not yet attract such incomers, and the injunction to be kind to the *gēr* had no practical relevance. In later times, the issue became a live one again.[27]

Despite the fact that the command to love the alien in their midst is the second most repeated commandment (other than to worship only one God),[28] Israel, like most cultures, had intense struggles in dealing with outsiders. A consistent tension exists in the text between the command to remember the deliverance from Egypt, thus providing for and welcoming the stranger, and the commitment to Yahwism resulting in exclusion of foreign peoples because of their religions and cultural practices. Caring for the stranger, the outcast, and the wholly dependent in society, however, is a pervasive theme in the Old Testament that translates directly into the ministry of Jesus in the New Testament. The theme survives into the ministries of the prophets, where a future, more universal faith in YHWH, brings foreigners into the fold of Israel (c.f. Ezek 47:21–23; Isa 14:1; 56:1–8).

Telling the Biblical Stories:
New Testament Life and Teaching

The Gospels do not directly teach on the subject of strangers, nor do they explicitly deal with the issue of migration or sojourning; however, the actions of Jesus in his ministry and the witness of early Christians presuppose an inclusive theology toward all outsiders. To begin, the narrative of Matthew paints Jesus as a refugee in Egypt fleeing the persecution of Herod, who sought to kill him (Matt 2:13–23). Jesus is described as a "divine immigrant" leaving the glories of the heavens to "live among us and save us on earth" (c.f. Phil 2:6–8).[29]

---

27. Maccoby, "Holiness and Purity," 169.

28. O'Neill, "Christian Hospitality and Solidarity with the Stranger,"149.

29. Soerens and Hwang, *Welcoming the Stranger*, 86.

Particularly, Jesus's call to minister to the outsider made many of his contemporaries uncomfortable. Take, for instance, Jesus's treatment of the Samaritans. The Samaritans practiced a form of Judaism (though explicitly rejecting the temple and holy sites of the Jews) but were not accepted as equals by Jews and often found themselves in bitter conflict with Jews living near them. The hostilities of the groups escalated in the early first century, just as Jesus was growing up in Nazareth, causing irreparable harm to the groups' relationship. Samaritans no longer were just "outsiders," but enemies. Still, Jesus engaged Samaritans on a number of occasions. John 4 shows that he met with a Samaritan woman at a well, offering her (a Samaritan, a woman, and an adulterer) entrance to the Kingdom of God.[30]

Jesus risked his own reputation to teach his disciples the importance of crossing the cultural and political boundaries with the message of God's kingdom. When asked by a shrewd lawyer, "Who is my neighbor?" in Luke 10, Jesus responds with the story of the Compassionate Samaritan, a story which underscores the faith of an outsider over against the faith of the priests and Levites in Israelite religion.[31] "Jesus lays aside the exclusivistic mores and negative feelings of his cultural heritage toward Samaritans for more important things: their value as persons and the potential of their faith."[32]

In addition, Jesus is painted as the ultimate gracious and inviting host, including those of all backgrounds and life situations (e.g., Matt 9:9–11, 15:31–33, 21:30–32; 26:25–27; Mark 2:14–16; Luke 14, 19:1–10; John 6:4–6). Most importantly, Jesus shared meals with outsiders—a central theme to most biblical stories of hospitality. In the "context of shared meals, the presence of God's Kingdom is prefigured, revealed, and reflected."[33] Jesus dined with many different kinds of people, challenging "the prevailing religious and cultural boundaries by the company he kept," exposing

30. Carroll R., 116–22.

31. Ibid.

32. Ibid., 125.

33. Pohl, *Making Room,* 30.

"the hidden patterns of social exclusion."[34] Jesus gathered at the homes of people with varied (often questionable) backgrounds: "Most writers now agree that eating with 'sinners' was one of the most characteristic and striking marks of Jesus's regular activity. . . . Jesus was, as it were, celebrating the messianic banquet, and doing so with all the wrong people."[35]

The great banquet depicted in Luke 14:7–24 at the Pharisee's house is a high point in the gospel that parallels the messianic feast described in Isa 25:6–9. Isaiah's messianic feast depicts all nations participating in the banquet without even bringing any gifts to honor Yahweh. In the Lukan parallel (vv. 7–14), Jesus gets upset as the guests vie for prominence and explains to the host "that the special guests at a banquet in God's sight would be the poor and the sick, those of no social standing who would not have the means to repay the gesture."[36] In verses 15–24, Jesus gives the host a parable about a host inviting his peers to a banquet. These invited guests may make excuses when they do not come, but the host (who has a change of heart as the empty excuses pour in), seeks to invite instead "the crippled, the blind, and the lame" (v.21)—those in the community with no social standing: outsiders. One scholar exegeted the passage thusly:

> The church is to participate actively in the life of the world as slaves and envoys of the true King, in a manner akin to Jesus, extending an invitation to those, like they were previously, who are not worthy guests, who are marginalized in the wider society, who do not consider themselves invited, and who have not even heard there is such a banquet available. Some will reject the invitation, others will accept, and some will need encouragement to believe that such an invitation includes them. The invitation is not to revelry or idolatry, but to the messianic feast that has already begun. Like Jesus, the speech and action of the church is simultaneously centrifugal—they

34. Ibid., 73.

35. Wright, *Jesus and the Victory of God*, 431.

36. Carroll R., 130.

go out into the world—and centripetal—the world is drawn into participating in the banquet.[37]

Jesus goes on in the Last Supper to fill the basic elements of a shared meal with symbolic meaning and instructed his followers to remember him likewise—at the table of hospitality and equality. At that table, "we remember the cost of our welcome, Christ's broken body and shed blood, [and] we also celebrate the reconciliation and relationship available to us because of his sacrifice and through his hospitality."[38] This is further repeated in Scripture in Jesus's post-resurrection encounter with the two disciples on the road to Emmaus (Luke 24:13–35). Jesus comes to the disciples as a stranger and is welcomed as a guest. In their sharing of table fellowship, the disciples recognize the risen Lord. Showing hospitality in breaking bread is an "anticipation of the Eucharist and a foretaste of the final Kingdom banquet."[39]

Early Church Hospitality

The early church followed the example of Jesus's welcome to others, and the epistles demonstrate the importance of hospitality in the daily lives of early believers:

> Paul instructs believers to practice or pursue hospitality (Rom 12:13), the writer of Hebrews reminds believers not to neglect hospitality (Heb 13:2), the author of 1 Peter challenges the community to offer hospitality ungrudgingly (1 Pet 4:9). Hospitality, in each of these passages, is a concrete expression of love—love for sisters and brothers, love extended outward to strangers, prisoners, and exiles, love that attends to physical and social needs . . . Hospitality is not optional for Christians, nor is it limited to those who are specially gifted for it. It is, instead, a necessary practice for the community of faith.[40]

37. Bretherton, *Hospitality as Holiness*, 135.

38. Pohl, *Making Room*, 30.

39. Ibid., 31.

40. Ibid.

In Greek, one of the key words used to describe this hospitality Christians were to practice is *philoxenia*, which is a combination of *phileo*, a general word for love or affection for people who are connected by kinship or faith, and *xenia*, the word for stranger. It is clearer in the Greek that this practice of hospitality is meant for strangers. Sometimes these strangers were other Christians needing assistance, but it is also clear that Christians were to show hospitality to the larger society as well (1 Thess 3:12; Gal 6:10).[41]

Hospitality toward others was practiced for theological reasons, but it also had a practical side. First, the early Christians, like all humanity, had to eat. Since the church "had all things in common" (Acts 2:44), they often shared meals. In the course of these shared meals, "tensions surfaced between rich and poor believers; meals provided the context for instructions on equal recognition and respect"[42] (Acts 10–11; Gal 2:11–14; 1 Cor 11:17–34; Jas 2:1–13). Second, the gospel spread through believers traveling widely and these missionaries depended on the hospitality of others to spread their message (Acts 16:14–15, 29–34; 18:1–3, 11; 28:30). Third, the early believers often met in households to worship, necessitating a gracious host, and fostering "family-like ties among believers . . . [providing] . . . a setting in which to shape and to reinforce a new identity."[43]

First Peter provides a beautiful description of Christians as sojourners (strangers) in the world. Whether this means that their citizenship is in heaven alone or that these Christians were considered foreigners in their land, they all became distinctly outsiders in their social location as followers of Jesus Christ and adherents to a new and distinct way of living.[44] These social outcasts mirror those immigrants, strangers, and outsiders living alone and isolated among the dominant culture, some with no faith community to serve them. Christians must continue to seek the vision of Christ and the Kingdom by reaching and ministering to these so-called

41. Ibid.
42. Ibid., 32.
43. Ibid.
44. Carroll R., 128–29.

"others," no matter the social cost; for, just as 1 Peter suggests: "Now who will harm you if you are eager to do what is good? But even if you do suffer for doing what is right, you are blessed" (1 Pet 3:13–14a). The early church embraced this alien status to further the gospel to all people:

> As members of God's household, Christians were to live as aliens in the world—aliens who practiced hospitality to strangers. Alien status suggested a framework for transformed loyalties and relationships, and a distinctive life-style for citizens of heaven who were simultaneously residents on earth . . . Offering care to strangers became one of the distinguishing marks of the authenticity of the Christian gospel and of the church. Writings from the first five centuries demonstrate the importance of hospitality in defining the church as a universal community, in denying the significance of the status boundaries and distinctions of the larger society, in recognizing the value of every person, and in providing practical care for the poor, stranger, and sick . . . We, like the early church, find ourselves in a fragmented and multicultural society that yearns for relationships, identity, and meaning.[45]

Despite the example of Jesus and the imitation of Christ by the early church, some passages in the New Testament struggle with the issue of authority over against radical action on behalf of others—just as Israel in the Old Testament struggled with the issue of migration and how to deal with foreigners. More conservative theology seeks to adhere to the current laws of a given nation-state based on specific theology derived from a few New Testament passages, effectively ignoring the radical stance of Jesus and the early church concerning strangers. For instance, Jesus speaks of paying taxes to Caesar (Matt 22:15–22) and confirms the authority of the Romans to levy taxes on Jews.[46] Additionally, Paul reinforces state authority in Romans 13, which some Christians assume means that all law is good and just and should be followed at all times.

45. Pohl, 32–33.

46. Though this too affirms that Jesus recognized a difference in Divine Authority and the Imperial Authority of Rome.

The problem with that narrow interpretation lies in the preceding chapter of Romans, where Paul "exhorts believers not to be shaped by the 'pattern of this world'; they should serve others, show love and have compassion, and help their enemies (Rom 12:3–21)."[47] Christians must accept that a government has a set of rules and seek to follow those rules; however, Christians must also measure those rules against their faith and convictions.

When laws are unjust and do not conform to the gospel, Christians have the responsibility to address them from a faith-based perspective, just as Jesus did in first-century Palestine. Jesus's gospel was radical and posed itself against the culturally accepted rules of his time; it held a *theological* basis for a *social* revolution that had as its mantra: "So the last will be first, and the first will be last" (Matt 20:16). This revolution was not a battleground for war, but a "calling into being cells of followers committed to his way of life."[48] This proclamation of a new kingdom, opposing armed resistance and calling into question the very grounds of the Jewish leaders' teaching, initiated an invitation and a challenge. Those who drop everything to follow Christ receive a summons, a call to duty, and should expect opposition, much like what Jesus faced in his ministry, yet are blessed with the peace of God for their service.[49] Simply put:

> Jesus does not resolve the tension between hospitality and holiness present in the Old Testament, but he does relate those two imperatives in a particular way. Jesus relates hospitality and holiness by inverting their relations: hospitality becomes the means of holiness. Instead of having to be set apart from or exclude pagans in order to maintain holiness, it is in Jesus's hospitality of pagans, the unclean, and sinners that his own holiness is shown forth. Instead of sin and impurity infecting him, it seems Jesus's purity and righteousness somehow 'infects' the impure, sinners, and the Gentiles . . . [and] Jesus's

47. Carroll R., 133.
48. Wright, 297.
49. Ibid., 298–304.

hospitality is not to be isolated to himself: he calls his disciples to 'Go and do likewise' (Lk 10:37).[50]

Conclusions Concerning Biblical Stories

The experience of the stranger is normative for the people of God in both the Old and New Testaments. The Israelites as well as the early Christians understood themselves to be aliens and sojourners as a reminder of their dependence on God. The Israelites knew what it was to be a stranger in a foreign land and were called to remember it in their treatment of the sojourner. The early church understood itself as alien to its culture (whether actually aliens in the countries where they resided or not). They had new loyalties and a new way of life, leading to a sharing of lives and a transcending of significant social and ethnic differences.[51] Moreover, early Christians sought to understand their hospitality within the context of understanding Jesus as both ultimate host and potential guest: "I was a stranger and you welcomed me" (Matt 25:35).

---

50. Bretherton, 131.
51. Pohl, 105.

3

Telling the Stories, Part II

Feminism and Stories

Feminism works to create space for everyone's voice, specifically seeking out the stories of those generally left unheard—both for women and for all marginalized people (the latter, with special gratitude to the hard work of Black Feminist Liberationist, *Mujeristas*, Womanists). Two of these traditions, Black Feminist Liberationist and *Mujerista,* provide excellent theological insights on Scripture, interpretation, and ways of seeing the text and context, while simultaneously examining the daily lives of the oppressed, their hopes and dreams, and their own ideas for changing the broken system that ensnares them.

Black Feminist and Liberationist Stories

Traci West's book *Disruptive Christian Ethics: When Racism and Women's Lives Matter* provides a Black Feminist Liberationist viewpoint, meaning her work not only hears the stories of the lives of the marginalized, but also pays special attention to the conditions that led to and continue to oppress them. She combines both theory and practice in her work: "Theory needs practice in order to be authentic, relevant, and truthful. Practice needs theory so that practices might be fully comprehended."[1] West insists that the marginalized be given space to tell their own stories in order to communicate well about topics of major importance. Thus, a dialogue between those considered great Christian ethicists (many of them white and male)[2] and the oppressed people themselves is necessary in order to fully grasp social situations for the most marginalized in society. Black feminist liberation theology like West's continues the feminist tradition of adjusting the emphasis on individual autonomy, drawing into conversation not only the fact that persons are individuals with freedom to make their own choices, but also that their relationships with others are of utmost importance both in understanding their successes and plights as well as in addressing issues. Problems are to be solved on a community level, not just an individual level:

> Autonomy and relationality are both inseparable and necessary for nurturing and confirming personhood (moral worth). When supposedly making our own choices, our dependent relationships to other persons and to the natural environment are at the center of how we learn, know, and experience what is moral and immoral. It is through these relationships that we even recognize the need for the freedom to make moral choices and come to learn what those choices might entail. Choices about exercising our freedom should infuse, enhance, or maintain respect in our relationships with one another.[3]

Black feminist thinkers like West look deeper into the lives of marginalized women to deflect the erroneous and debasing caricatures played out in Congress and the media. Challenging the way the poor and marginalized have been treated is no easy task.

1. Traci C. West, *Disruptive Christian Ethics*, xvii. Black Feminist Liberationist thought, while specific to the black community, applies widely to women of color and the struggles they face. Feminist thought is never meant to be narrowly construed as applicable to only one subset of people, but as a rallying cry for all to listen to the marginalized, let them speak for themselves, know their stories, and move into a place of solidarity with them.

2. Ibid., 4.

3. Ibid., 63.

This is a re-writing of cultural history and demands strong and persistent voices speaking against ignoring the actual narratives of the oppressed. When U.S. Christians consider whether to democratically support policy initiatives restricting immigration status or making it harder to obtain, the perspective of those receiving (or not receiving) the benefits should matter a great deal. That kind of openness to the eyewitness testimony of the poor and marginalized "generates an uneasiness that lingers" for those "focused upon defending the moral fiber of [the] poor . . . even defenders seem to be caught identifying people who are poor as having [a] problem that needs to be addressed"[4] rather than simply allowing the stories of the oppressed to guide the conversation. It takes courage and humility to step away from society's presumptions and really listen.

West makes important theological connections to re-characterize how best to hear and understand the stories of the marginalized poor, based in her reading of the Scripture passage that is commonly referred to as "Mary's Magnificat" in the first chapter of the Gospel of Luke. West claims, as I have, that Christian Scripture concerns itself with stories of faith as people grappled with challenging social and political realities. In the case of Mary of Nazareth's "song" prior to the birth of Jesus Christ, her son, West claims that Mary's words, as recorded in Luke 1:46a-55 are actually theological pronouncements about power that challenge us regarding our treatment of the marginalized by teaching a moral lesson about wealth and poverty and offering a "radical theological understanding of political realities that create these inequalities."[5]

Considering the words of the unwed, pregnant Mary in the first century over against the problems of the current state welfare functioning in the twenty first century, West attempts to show that moral lessons gleaned from this passage can assist with a better understanding the plight of poor women now. While her focus may be on the problems of a lack of welfare offered to those women most vulnerable, with children to care for and little to no

4. Ibid.

5. Ibid., 76.

family support, her words are helpful for understanding why all of the marginalized must be heard and how Black feminist theology can bolster the argument that women and minorities deserve space to speak for themselves. Luke's gospel, like most ancient texts, is fraught with social depictions of poor women that offend our sensibilities in modern times, but despite this, West insists that Mary's words in the Magnificat "carry a message about God's concern for the particular lives and needs of the lowly and poor . . . [that] stresses God's powerful actions on their behalf."[6]

First, there must be a *blessing of the particular*. Mary's Magnificat speaks of particular circumstances and lowly status, especially that of poor, unwed mothers (a group of especially marginalized persons both in the first century and now). The plight of particular circumstances like poverty matters to God, who provides salvation for the poor and oppressed. Second, there must be *no more humiliation*. Mary has "triumphed over her enemies." Victory in God's mercy should lead contemporary marginalized people to salvation and justice, just as it did for Mary. This means no more privileged tolerance of marginalized people's suffering and indifference to their situations. Third, *reversal* must occur. By this, West means that Mary's Magnificat and her particular situation are linked "with God's delivery of justice in the broader society."[7] This delivery of justice comes about as part of a reversal of situations: instead of regulating the poorest and most destitute, the wealthy and powerful become the more regulated (such as by having their morality analyzed and probed with the same close scrutiny given to that of the poor and marginalized).[8] Lastly, she emphasizes the concept of *churches breaking their primary allegiance to the state's agenda*. Churches asked to provide government services must be able to separate ethically from the state-sanctioned illegitimacy attributed to their parishioners, including not only the poor or persons of color, but also those denied by law the right to even be present in the country. Churches instead should call for changes in

6. Ibid., 82.
7. Ibid., 106–7.
8. Ibid.

how the problems are solved. White U.S. citizen Christians must resist the comfort they can find in supporting values that point to the superiority of their own racial group. When undocumented, poor families who need benefit of better immigration laws are depicted as having a cracked foundation and innate tendencies toward criminality, white, U.S. citizens receive the unearned reward of being excluded from this depiction. If Christians can adjust their theology to one that blesses persons in the particular and sees injustice and God's power of salvation over it through their eyes, contemporary stories that mirror Mary's Song will help bring the outcasts back into community and the privileged to a place of solidarity.

Mujeristas Luchando Por Voz/ Mujeristas Fighting for a Voice

Ya las gentes murmuran que yo soy tu enemiga
porque dicen que en verso doy al mundo mi yo.
Mienten, Julia de Burgos. Mienten, Julia de Burgos.
La que se alza en mis versos no es tu voz: es mi voz
porque tú eres ropaje y la esencia soy yo; y el más
profundo abismo se tiende entre las dos.

Already the people murmur that I am your enemy
because they say that in verse I give your I to the world.
They lie, Julia de Burgos. They lie, Julia de Burgos
who rises in my verses is not your voice. It is my voice
because you are the dressing and the essence is I;
and the most profound abyss is spread between us.[9]

One's story, her own truth, must come from her own voice. No one else can tell it the way she tells it. No one can create others'

---

9. "A Julia de Burgos," quoted and translated by Ada María Isasi-Díaz, *La Lucha Continues: Mujerista Theology,* 195–96. Original Source: Julia de Burgos, *Song of the Simple Truth.*

narratives and produce truth, for the honesty of one's own story cannot be duplicated by someone else's interpretation of a life: "What rises in my verses is not your voice. It is my voice because you are the dressing and the essence is I; and the most profound abyss is spread between us."[10] Truth, for this poet, is in her voice as woman without boundaries, while the lie is the mask of a person put forth by her conventional roles of mother, wife, and object. The voice is buried beneath how others view her. The voice is her truth, her *I*, her story. To hear her truth, not only must she see beyond her own artificial limitations as a woman in a specific kind of culture, but so must her listeners.

Mujerista theology is a theology of story and real life based in Latina/Hispana culture that focuses on grassroots understandings of actual lived stories, rather than beginning theology with theory. *Mujerista* theology is a subset of liberation theology, with a more specific focus on giving voice to Latinas/Hispanas. *Mujeristas* focus on the participation of those who suffer, especially poor women of Latin/Hispanic heritage. Their *proyecto histórico* (historical project) expands beyond that posed by Liberation theologians, aiming toward a specific liberation of women in their day-to-day struggle to survive.[11] They embrace the work of liberation theology that places preference on the poor and marginalized, but go a step further to experience alongside women of Latina and Hispanic heritage their own lived daily experiences. By incorporating stories and feelings, these theologians seek to build bridges between the Hispana/Latina communities to link to those who differ from them by sharing their liberative stories.

Ana María Isasi-Díaz's book *La Lucha Continues* (The Fight Continues) leads with this focus on story—the author's own narrative of the daily life of a Latina/Hispana woman. The rest of the book is dedicated to explicating the function of the different aspects of *mujerista* theology, such as *lo cotidiano* (the everyday), social location, difference, liberating culture, *burlando al opresor* (tricking the oppressor, creating a new future shaped by Hispana/

10. Ibid.

11. Isasi-Díaz, "Defining our *Proyecto Histórico*," 120.

Latina women), justice and love, and reconciliation. Through her own transformation into feminist scholar, then shaper of *mujerista* theology, Isasi-Díaz has become one of the stronger voices contributing to the important work of bringing about changes that give voice to Latina/Hispana women in the United States. Isasi-Díaz writes her own story of when she recognized the lack of voice given to women in the Roman Catholic Church, and from within began to ask questions of the leadership from a grassroots group of Women of Color (WOC). One of the main goals for Isasi-Díaz was bringing light to the power being used to dominate and cover up the voices of Latina/Hispana women in the Church, and in doing so, she realized not only that poverty was an issue, but that sexism instead of being separate from it, compounded it, resulting in even less of a voice for the marginalized women for and with whom she advocated. Appeals to justice simply are not enough, she writes; *narratives* must be told to create a bridge between the experience of lived reality and political arguments about justice. For Hispanas/Latinas, Isasi-Díaz writes that the ongoing revelation of God manifests itself in *lo cotidiano* (the everyday), as well as the bodily actions of both thinking and being in the world. The goal of liberation leads to reflective praxis that involves action, decision, and interaction with the world. And no decision occurs without emotion.[12]

Oftentimes, emotion is not seen as a positive element of morality,[13] but Isasi-Díaz posits that "To know reality . . . one has to

12. Isasi-Díaz, *La Lucha Continues,* 51.

13. Martha Nussbaum in her book *Sex and Social Justice,* pp.72–73, discusses reason and emotion in her section on the feminist critique of liberalism. She deduces that some liberal thinkers have concluded erroneously that emotions hold an inferior status to reason (or are "confused reasoning") because emotions have long been understood as "female" and thus inherently of lesser importance to a male-dominated discipline. But, as Nussbaum points out, emotions can be a function of reason; emotive responses like grief and fear are both ways of seeing and understanding. Liberal thinkers have not all dismissed the value of emotion, and though the strand of liberal ethics lacks coherency, feminist critique can offer ways to improve upon the liberal tradition by experiencing the value of emotional attachments by recognizing that emotions are part of cognition and thus should be evaluated positively. Additionally, though

be, first of all, enmeshed in a situation, one has to be impacted and affected by it."[14] The emotion of people's stories is what *Mujerista* theology leans on. One can only really become involved materially in a situation by feeling those things which the marginalized feel: "The anguish, pain, fright, and loss we [feel] can very well be placed at the service of making us go beyond our regular pattern of analyzing and dealing with situations in which we place ourselves always at the center." [15] When we hear the stories of the oppressed and marginalized from their own mouths, when we start to feel their pains as our own by listening to their personal stories, fraught with emotion, only then can we begin to change our views about those persons we would normally keep at arms-length, including Latinas/Hispanas and all those oppressed and seeking justice. No longer are we simply dealing in our rational/cost-benefit analysis, but we are going beyond ourselves into the lives of those without our privilege. Emotions can guide us away from the "objectivity" of the supposed impartiality of non-emotive thinking and reasoning. "Pure reason" so often overpowers the pain of those under power, domination, and control. This supposed objectivity, according to *mujeristas*, is simply "the subjectivity of those who have the power to impose their own point of view on others."[16]

Instead of being a roadblock to reason, emotions are a way of understanding reality that is inherent to the human condition. To be sure, emotions must be in concert with reason to some extent, but reason without emotion is not only disingenuous; it is harmful. Humans experience the world through both intellect and feeling. The gut-wrenching sensations in the face of injustice are part of the drive to then use intellect and emotions together to solve

---

some stronger feminist critiques would assert that emotion cannot contain the kind of reason liberalism espouses, even the most self-giving of persons is involved in evaluative thinking in their emotion-giving, and if she is not involved in that, she is being taken advantage of by giving of herself to her own detriment and without care for the self. This lack of distinguishing of her own well-being from that of others is where the problem lies.

14. Isasi-Díaz, *La Lucha Continues*, 110.

15. Ibid., 112.

16. Ibid., 213.

problems. Isasi-Díaz insists that without emotions, "our knowledge is incomplete, our understanding is severely hampered, our reasoning is faulty."[17] Internalizing stories allows the emotions of the marginalized to spur us to hear them in ways some supposed "pure intellect" cannot. Additionally, trusting emotions becomes important for the privileged. No longer is an injustice a matter of supposedly emotionless analysis; it becomes instead a human situation requiring a fully human response, empathizing with the marginalized's feelings while simultaneously allowing them to use their own emotions as a driving force for change on their parts.

Instead of providing a "one size fits all" strategy for all Latinas/Hispanas, Isasi-Díaz calls for recognizing the differences in the daily lives of the oppressed while also seeing the "empathetic fusion" of their shared experiences. The stories from those most affected by social structures in the United States must be heard to thoroughly explore any political/social issue that affects Hispanics/Latinos/Latinas in a way that culminates in justice. Doing this requires ongoing reflection on, anger toward, and changing of norms that keep whole groups marginalized.[18]

Listening to the Stories of Undocumented Immigrants

Working in the fields of immigration law and ministry, I have had the profound opportunity to meet, work with, and learn from, immigrants with stories. While much of my professional work in immigration law has been focused on corporate law, the cases that touch my heart most deeply are family-based and often deal with undocumented immigrants and their families doing everything possible to find a way to stay in the United States legally. These cases come with powerful stories that challenge me to re-evaluate my assumptions and intersect with my desire to love my neighbor. These cases reveal my ever-growing understanding of the

17. Ibid., 110.
18. Ibid., 213.

shortcomings of our current immigration legal system and confront me with the harder questions of immigration law. No longer are the concepts of the law simply a theoretical problem—they have a face, a life, a family. Similarly, as a minister, I have become acutely aware of people's needs in ways I had never imagined, and I have been given opportunities to serve with those on the front lines of the immigration debate as they encounter *lo cotidiano* (the everyday) lives of those caught up in a system beyond their grasp. Let us hear together a few of these stories.

Early in my career in immigration law, I worked on a pro bono case involving Cecilia,[19] a young, undocumented, Mexican mother of two young boys who had been sponsored for permanent residence by her husband, who was also a permanent resident. Because the process of sponsorship can take years for Mexican nationals married to permanent residents, Cecilia had been left without legal immigration recourse when her husband abused her. In fact, during the repeated abuse, her husband had called into question Cecilia's own morality, which is one of the discretionary ways permanent residence can be denied. He had called the police on her when she defended herself, falsely reporting *her* as the abuser to local police. None of this was her fault. It was his substance abuse, his threats of violence with a gun, his beating of his own elder son—yet here stood Cecilia, straddling the fence of finally being free of her husband through divorce and holding very little hope of finally gaining legal status once the divorce was finalized. Her two boys, born in the United States, and thus both U.S. citi-

---

19. Names changed to protect confidentiality in all of the following stories. I am grateful to have encountered some of these stories first-hand, as well as second-hand through my contacts at a local healthcare ministry serving the immigrant community. These stories are accounts of just a few of the ways immigrants are struggling in the U.S., and though more work could be done with case study analysis, this book only allows for a space of a few representative anecdotes to give a small glimpse into the struggles of the undocumented immigrant communities in the United States today. Stories must be told and heard, and these will serve only to begin the conversations as thoughtful Christians begin to listen to their immigrant neighbors more faithfully. There are many, many more stories to hear, and I hope these will encourage us all to listen to more of them regularly in our daily lives.

zens, would continue to run the risk of having their mother pulled away from them and deported. Cecilia stood in our office, having reached out through a nonprofit agency, with a pending divorce, almost no money, and now a husband who had made good on his threat to pull away her immigration status when she was most vulnerable. "Standing in line" for immigration benefits for Cecilia was not so simple—it would mean staying with her abuser, keeping her boys near someone who threatened their life and health. But thankfully, at least for that term, Congress had reauthorized the Violence Against Women Act or VAWA, which allows abused spouses to petition the United States Citizenship and Immigration Services (USCIS, formerly known as the Immigration and Naturalization Service, or INS) for residence after demonstrating (with copious amounts of paper and a definite need for a legal team) that he or she qualifies based on the history of abuse and that he or she has good moral character (which can be hard to overcome when abusers routinely lie about their spouse to authorities). Because of countless pro bono hours, Cecilia's impassioned statement, the statements of her two struggling boys, the statements of witnesses of the abuse and his alcoholism—along with just enough evidence to convince the USCIS officer, Cecilia was finally fully free of her abuser. No longer required to have him as a sponsor, she could remain in the U.S. to care for her two boys on her own terms. Her story is one of the happy endings, leading to an eventual arrest of her ex-husband, with his admission to guilt of abusing his spouse in open court. Hers is a story of courage in the face of fear, persistence when all hope seemed lost. I was grateful then, and for cases since, where legal avenues like VAWA exist, but it left me wondering then and now—what if Cecilia had had options to enter legally to begin with? What if she had already been working here legally and able to support her children alone? What if laws designed to prevent illegal entry had not backfired and made her remain here for fear of being barred from entry for ten years? Why is it so easy to be sponsored by an abuser and so hard to get away from it? Why were there no more options for Cecilia and her boys? And why, just a few years later, did it take Congress so long to re-authorize

such a basic protective law as VAWA by politicizing it as some sort
of anti-family values bill? I was hard-pressed then and now to understand the logic behind those 22 dissenting votes.[20]

A young couple, Pablo and Susanna, had married in rural
Tennessee at a small Baptist church. Their friends and family were
excited for their future. Pablo was a strong worker and labored
as a brick layer for many years and had recently felt the call of
God on his life to begin working in ministry at his church. The
pair were inseparable, and just a year into their marriage, they
welcomed a sweet little girl, Lily, into their family. But behind
all of their outward joy, there was the lingering knowledge that
Pablo, who had arrived in the United States as a teenager many
years ago and had crossed the border more than once, would not
be eligible to become a permanent resident just because he had
married Susanna, a U.S. citizen. Unlike cases where an immigrant
has only entered the U.S. one time and accrued unlawful presence
(which is forgivable when an immigrant is becoming a resident
based on marriage to a citizen), Pablo would have to leave the
United States and process for an immigrant visa at the U.S. consulate in Juarez, Mexico—waiting for months, even years, in one of
the most violent cities in the world. His case could not have been
approved immediately, as he would have to present evidence of
"extreme hardship" to his U.S. citizen family members if he were
not allowed to become a permanent resident (a requirement not
easily met). This young family, their pastor, and Susanna's parents
all sat around our boardroom table, explaining how wonderful
Pablo had been in the community and church, and all fearful and
worried about what to do next. They did not want Pablo to keep
having to hide, but exposing him to the legal immigration process
could have him deported or stuck in Mexico for up to ten years.
For months, our immigration team worked with the family and
their friends to gather evidence of hardship. Honest and conservative rural Tennesseans wrote letters explaining their unease about
supporting someone "breaking the law," but knowing Pablo, they
felt compelled to try to help. This immigrant—he was different:

20. Ball, "Why Would Anyone Oppose the Violence Against Women Act?"

59

"We know him. He is good people." (Stories and the intersection of lives are strong motivators for change). With so many support letters and evidence of depression and anxiety for his wife, we sent Pablo to the consulate armed with all he could muster. The consulate took his papers and sent him away. He waited weeks and weeks, working odd jobs at an English-speaking resort just outside Juarez. When the consulate issued a notice stating that the evidence was not enough, the family once again jumped into action, preparing everything they could. Susanna personally flew to Mexico to submit it with Pablo. They waited. Months passed. The family was constantly in tears and worried. Susanna could not remain in Mexico, fearful for her child's safety, and Pablo would not have it anyway—he could not ask them to stay. Susanna returned to the United States with Lily and sat anxiously awaiting news, spending countless hours crying with her parents and on the phone with her husband, who seemed a world away. After over a year of waiting, the case was finally approved. Pablo could re-enter the U.S. and rejoin his family and community. So few hardship cases are approved, though, and most families do not want to risk the long separation. The extension of DAPA by the executive branch, mentioned in the first chapter, would have allowed immigrants like Pablo to process their cases while staying in the U.S. with their families, many of them U.S. citizens, rather than spending months or years in their home country, surrounded by the very violence they fled from years ago. But this executive order has been fought fiercely by those seeking to slow or even end immigration to the United States and is currently under review in the courts, with its regulations on hold and unavailable to families like Pablo's until the court makes a decision, which could still be years away.

Immigrants also face fraudsters seeking to make money off their desperate desire to find a legal pathway to residence or citizenship. One client, Héctor, presented his birth certificate to a *notario* early in his time in the United States. It was about 1995, and Héctor and his brother had sneaked into the U.S. at the Texas border and moved to Georgia to find work. They wanted to find a way to legally stay in the country, so they sought help from a *notario* claiming to be able to provide immigration legal help. *Notarios publicos* are trained legal professionals in Spanish-speaking countries, so when Spanish-speaking immigrants encounter them in the United States, they feel as if they are going to get the legal help they need. But in the United States, *notarios* are notorious. U.S. notaries are only state-commissioned officials with narrow witnessing duties (think a notary at a bank witnessing a signing of a mortgage document and stamping it with a state-issued seal), yet these *notarios* (a similar word with a very different meaning), pass themselves off as immigration consultants. In reality, though, they are practicing law without a license and often are in their business for profit, not to actually assist immigrants. Their claim is that they can assist with residence at a lower cost than an attorney, but often they steal information and take money without ever actually helping any of their clients.[21] Thus, when Héctor presented his birth certificate and then did not receive the help he paid for, he wrote it off as a mistake and just kept working his job in Georgia. For nearly fifteen years, he toiled away in manual labor, and in 2008, he met and married a lovely woman, a native of Honduras, whose parents had come to the U.S. many years ago as religious workers. She and her parents had all naturalized together over ten years before she married Héctor. Thus, Héctor's U.S. citizen wife worked to file the papers for him through a nonprofit Spanish-speaking service group that is a Board of Immigration Appeals-certified preparer of immigration documents. These well-trained employees had prepared everything correctly. Everything seemed in order and straightforward for this family. Héctor's unlawful presence would be forgiven, as he had only sneaked in one time, and within a few months, Héctor would be living and working legally in the United States. The case was denied. The preparers and Héctor were shocked and looking for answers. USCIS did not give much reason why—only that Héctor had apparently been deported in 1996. Of course, Héctor knew he had never been deported, and thus his

21. For more information on *notario* fraud, please see: Thun, "'Notario Publico' And Notary Fraud," of the National Notary Association, or the American Bar Association's Fight Notario Fraud Project.

case was given to one of our attorneys. Our team spent weeks requesting evidence from USCIS using the Freedom of Information Act. When Héctor's immigration file finally arrived, the full story was uncovered. The *notario* in 1995 had sold Héctor's birth certificate to another man who then used Héctor's identity to apply for asylum, which was denied (for good reason—the application was near-blank and clearly not approvable). This unnamed man was then flagged for deportation, never found, and the deportation hearing he did not attend left the real Héctor unable to become a resident. It took our office countless hours, billing our time only partially to this very poor family, to finally clear his record. Héctor, without an experienced immigration attorney's help (an attorney who helpfully used to work for USCIS and had many contacts at the various agencies), would likely never have cleared his name. Fraudsters could have easily had the last word for a family just trying to stay together. Thankfully, he did find an attorney, and thankfully, with much pressure and loads of evidence of Héctor's whereabouts for the last fifteen years, Héctor finally adjusted his status to permanent residence and can remain with his wife and two small children in north Georgia.

So many immigrants face these legal restrictions and fraudsters every day; there are a countless stories of families torn apart, trying to find legal avenues and finding none. These families do not want to remain here without status and are actively seeking to legalize their status and be a part of the American Dream. They face more fear and anxiety every day than the average white, U.S. citizen can even imagine—just due to their lack of immigration status. In ministry, I have encountered even more stories of struggle, focused not just on the legal realities for families, but their anxieties and social struggles as well. In one local ministry-sponsored healthcare provider for those under the federal poverty line who have no health insurance, the stories are wide and varied. My own participation in the stories and lives of these immigrants is one of observation, but the realities mark the lives of those who work with the immigrants on a daily basis, from the medical volunteers to the staff social workers. This Richmond, Virginia-based ministry is one of the few places in the city to be treated and not judged for their immigration status (or lack thereof), and it tends to the health and welfare of a myriad of immigrants and refugees. The staff and volunteers who minister there have encountered whole families of struggling immigrants, some who have sneaked in under great pressure to remove themselves from scary situations abroad, and some who have been here for years, isolated by their immigrant status and lack of English skills. Most do not qualify for any form of government assistance for healthcare or food, and even those with U.S. citizen children face poverty and malnourishment out of fear of reaching out for support for their children, who are entitled to assistance. The basic stressors of daily living come with a constant dose of fear and anxiety.

In the past year or so, the ministry has received a number of undocumented adolescents into their care who have crossed the border by themselves. One such teen, Mariana, crossed the U.S. border alone, fleeing Honduras' violence, at the tender age of sixteen. She was apprehended by border agents and held at an immigration detention center. Eventually her estranged father, who had been living in the United States for some time, came forward to claim her and supposedly take her into his home. But the father had no intention of caring for her. Her older brother Juan, a teenager himself at only 18 years old, and a dish washer at a local chain restaurant, could not offer enough to care for her either, though he certainly tried. The father was the guardian, but only on paper; Mariana was on her own. She went to the local high school and made a friend, Gabriela, who had also crossed the border on her own some years before. Gabriela's mother received her healthcare at the ministry, and when the mother realized what was going on with Mariana, she brought the girl to see the ministry's social worker. It was February on the mid-Atlantic coast, and despite the 20 degree temperatures, Mariana was in flip flops and a tank top; she owned no winter clothes. The ministry has been attempting to assist Mariana and her brother ever since, by both providing the necessities to live as well as pointing her to the legal help she needs. But without comprehensive immigration reform, Mariana may be stuck in immigration status limbo while struggling to find food, shelter, and appropriate clothing.

Another struggle for the staff with newly-arrived adolescents presents itself as young people, eager to help their families, are not accustomed to education. In their home countries, they likely had already dropped out of school before the end of elementary or middle school, so classes have not been a part of their lives since their young childhood, if at all. One such young man, Guillermo, arrived in the U.S. from Honduras at age fifteen, and now, at age sixteen, has been cited for truancy and processed in the juvenile court system, as Virginia law requires him to be enrolled and in attendance at school until age eighteen. After weeks of skipping school while being enrolled, he has been sent to court, along with his struggling mother. All he wants to do is to work to support his mother; he hates class and feels useless to his poverty-stricken family when he sits in classrooms unable to keep up with the lessons. He finds himself more useful earning a paycheck at a local company doing manual labor. Guillermo wakes at the crack of dawn each day for his job, packs his own lunch, works hard all day, and comes home to help his mother with chores and paying bills. But not being eighteen yet, he cannot legally choose to do that. The mother, at her wits end with court dates, has been trying to explain to him through the social worker that this choice to skip school and keep working affects her too—she may have more money to pay bills, but she ends up spending it on court fees to defend herself and her son. But Guillermo continues to feel like school is pointless—he is behind academically and embarrassed by his struggles. He knows he can be useful at a job and is more dedicated than most kids his age.

In addition to caring for the health and welfare of adolescents, the ministry hosts a prenatal care clinic for expecting moms. These mothers often complain of being judged at the local department of health clinics. Their choice to have more children despite their poverty, or their being pregnant when they arrive in the U.S., leads nurses and caregivers to press them to use birth control they do not fully understand or shames them for having become pregnant without a spouse. One Honduran teenager, seven months pregnant with twins, and her sister with a ten-month-old baby, crossed the border to join their mother in the U.S. Amazingly, they all arrived safely and the young mother delivered her twins at a high risk clinic in town. The details of the twins' father are unclear, but the safety of the teen and her kids was a concern when they chose to flee their home country. Now the mother and father of the girls, their two daughters, and now three grandbabies, along with another cousin, are all living under one roof—and suddenly a manageable situation has become unmanageable on their salaries. There are never enough groceries; kids are sleeping on the floor. They do not have enough clothing or diapers for the babies. They need rental assistance and an immigration attorney for the daughters. The money isn't available through state funds, and the ministry must rely on donations from local nonprofits and pro-bono attorneys to assist in their journey toward legal status using the long, arduous process of seeking asylum.

Many of the women in the prenatal program have a history of trauma and abuse and then come to the U.S. where they are socially isolated. They have no transportation (often paying someone for a ride to the doctor, but not being able to afford anything else). Their opportunities to meet other people are limited. They may have older children in their home country who are living with grandparents there. Their hearts are broken that they had to flee and leave behind innocent children to whom they can no longer be a parent. With low-paying jobs and little opportunity, they always feel like they cannot send enough money back, and often they do not have the resources to bring them here. Their guilt is palpable to the staff, and depression screenings can go but so far— only the most troubled can be put into nonprofit programs to get assistance. Even though nearly a third of these pregnant women score high enough on the screening to need mental healthcare, the ministry cannot help all of them, only assisting about a third of those top-scoring women. Traumatized by pregnancy and coming from Honduras, El Salvador, Guatemala, Mexico, Brazil, and Venezuela—all places of great violence—these women are barely able to make ends meet, much less take the necessary steps to heal (which often costs too much money and time to be feasible). If and when their older kids do arrive from the fearful circumstances the mother has fled, new challenges arise. Suddenly, the mother must redefine the relationship with the child who has been raised by other family members and may have felt abandoned. The mother must learn about her child, with whom she has had little chance to interact over the last few years. With a new family in the U.S., and the adjustment of her newly-arrived child to their new home, these women are desperate for a sense of normalcy, but they generally cannot get the help they need to sort out the complex emotions they face.

The undocumented visiting the clinic sometimes are applying for asylum and other legalization, and are in legal limbo waiting for their cases to be adjudicated by USCIS. Their wait period used to be spent largely in immigration detention centers, but in a recent (and in my assessment, misguided) attempt to reunite families, immigration officials have begun to release from prison those who previously would have been in detention waiting for adjudication—with one caveat—the immigrant must wear an ankle monitor. While ankle monitors have long been in use by prison systems for those accused of violent crimes out on bail, their use is relatively new for immigrants released from detention, the majority of whom do not have a criminal record of any kind, having only broken civil immigration law. In 2015, *The New York Times* published two exposé pieces on the use of what Spanish speakers call *grilletes* (the Spanish word for "shackles"). In it, the plight of mothers and their children released from detention centers only to be monitored by GPS is examined for the stigmatizing and largely unnecessary alternative it is to immigration detention:

> According to statistics released this year by a division of the Department of Homeland Security, nearly 90 percent of detained families expressing fear of returning to their home countries passed an initial screening for asylum eligibility. Now that those families are free to make their cases in the immigration court system, they have "every

incentive" to attend their hearings, said Elora Mukher-
jee, a professor at Columbia Law School who represents
families in Dilley.[22]

With prevalent backlogs on processing cases, even for those with a
pathway to legal status, the wait can take months or years, meaning
families, most of whom have no ties to crime other than that they
are fleeing it by entering the U.S., are being treated as if they have
committed the same crimes for which others with ankle monitors
have—thieves, rapists, even murderers. The other caveat is that
the government outsources the tracking to for-profit companies
even while ICE continues to do the check-ins for those wear-
ing the monitors. While the rules for the monitors preclude use
on pregnant women,[23] the imperfect nature of outsourcing and
poor training for agents has left a number of pregnant women in
precarious situations. At the prenatal clinic, one mother begged
her social worker to not keep her past a certain time during her
depression screening. If she arrived late to her check-in with the
agent, she would be treated badly, yelled at, and perhaps even detained again. It took weeks for her ankle monitor to be removed,
despite her pregnancy.

Sometimes the move to the U.S. is economic, or partly economic, for families. But more often than not, there is also a history
of trauma or fear of violence at home. Often they do not qualify for
refugee status, and on occasion are told to request asylum, but only
if they encounter a social worker or someone else familiar with the
legal options available to them. Very few groups here in my city,
perhaps just a handful of attorneys, are available for these kinds of
cases. Many have little to no Spanish language help. Besides, these
families cannot pay for groceries and rent, much less legal fees—
even if they are eligible for asylum. And attorneys, too, cannot be
pro bono indefinitely without help from outside funding.

22. Gogolak, "Ankle Monitors Weigh on Immigrant Mothers Released
from Detention."

23. Turkewitz, "Immigrant Mothers Released From Holding Centers, but
With Ankle Monitors."

Living as an undocumented immigrant in the United States comes with intense fear and anxiety. Any time immigrants encounter a police car or hear a siren—they are terrified, not knowing if this is an ICE officer coming to pull apart their family, the one stronghold they have in this new country. These undocumented immigrants struggle to ask for help and need places to go that feel safe. Families with small children are afraid to apply for food stamps—relying on public assistance could come back to bite them later, even if they are currently entitled, because applications for citizenship ask about this. Meeting basic needs and accessing services is quite different if one has no legal status here. Families cannot go to mainstream avenues for help, so social workers and staff at the clinic have to think creatively, and they must know the places that will or will not accept an immigrant without status. For instance, if someone goes to the emergency room in our city, one set of hospitals has assistance for fees for anyone of any immigration status, but another set of hospitals does not have assistance programs for undocumented immigrants. At this second set of hospitals, an undocumented immigrant will be saddled with a large bill and no financial assistance. When in need of housing and utility assistance, these families cannot find relief through HUD funding or other kinds of government assistance. If a family is about to become homeless, a social worker must know to refer the family to the right charity (in our case, to Central Intake at Catholic Charities) to find short-term housing. If undocumented, Central Intake is only a band aid and cannot help long-term. For utility and rental assistance, only the Salvation Army and sometimes Catholic Charities (because no ID is required, usually) will look the other way in regard to immigration status. All others will categorically deny services to any undocumented family a family, even one with U.S. citizen children. So, most of these families must rely on the charity of family and friends, and sometimes local churches (though even some local churches refuse to help those without immigration status—thankfully, the church I serve is not one of these).

And, as with any changing demographic, the immigrant community is beginning to face new challenges. Since immigration reforms were passed making it illegal to reenter the U.S. after sneaking in, many immigrants have simply remained in the U.S. with no status for decades. With no legal recourse, they have now aged and are becoming dependent, but with little in the way of assistance from outside sources. Once such family at the clinic faced a horrible revelation in regard to aging without immigration status. María and her husband Tomás, an elderly couple from Mexico, had lived in the Richmond area for three decades. During that time, María had raised three children and dealt with her husband's abusive tendencies. She had managed to deal with his verbal and physical abuse for many years, but in his old age, he began to develop dementia, and his abuse was getting worse. He became irrationally jealous about things that were not happening. She finally overcame her fears and filed a report with adult protective services. The agency got involved and did an assessment, but then abruptly closed the case. They could do nothing for her because of her lack of immigration status. Her family would have to be responsible for her safety, making sure someone was home with her at all times. After much searching, and with the help of many caring social workers and charities, María and her family finally received a reprieve through the generosity of others, having Tomás admitted to a local nursing home. But it was a long and drawn-out process that left María in grave danger in her own home for months—something that would not have occurred had María and her husband simply had immigration status.

Hearing All the Stories Together

In Scripture, we see the hard work of the Hebrews and Christians following God's commands to love and include the stranger and the marginalized. Then, in the work of Black Feminist Liberationist and *Mujerista* thought, Christians can begin to see how to listen to and understand those who are on the margins through their own stories. But simply knowing the scriptural basis for hospitality and love of the stranger is not enough. While beginning to learn to sit and listen to the stories of the marginalized is meaningful and definitely a great place to start for Christians, the realities of life on the margins have deeper roots than any one story can possibly convey. Thus, privileged white, U.S. citizen Christians here in the United States, after hearing stories and finding conviction among the lived realities of others, have more work to do. Not only should Christians understand the broken laws and hear (and really listen) to the stories of their immigrant neighbors; they also should begin to open their eyes to new ways of seeing the underlying moral brokenness that leads to the kind of politicking from which these laws emerge. It is essential that Christians see and understand structural evil, their own privilege, and the myriad of ways marginalization can occur.

4

Recognizing the Realities

UNDERSTANDING THE BASICS OF white privilege helps us to understand the systemic problems of racism and marginalization. While we will delve deeper into the topic of privilege in the next chapter, it is appropriate to consider it here briefly as we unpack the realties faced by the marginalized. The perpetuation of privilege continues legacies of domination that oftentimes those of us with privilege do not even notice. Access to power and resources are extremely limited for those minorities harmed by systems of oppression deeply rooted in historical racism. The problems of white supremacy, or white dominance, are characterized by the access to these resources by the privileged over against the lack of access by minorities and those without power. Feminist ethics has long recognized the power structures undergirding patriarchy, but the work of Black feminists, Womanists, and *Mujeristas* has uncovered an even larger legacy of power against those who are both minority and female. For these, we uncover not only the legacy of patriarchy, but the legacy of white dominance and its relationship to privilege. Privilege, as the manifestation of white dominance, is supported by many ingrained cultural systems of injustice that are so much a part of our cultural heritage it can be difficult to even notice them if one already has privilege.[1] This again is where listening, seeing, and working alongside those without privilege

1. West, *Disruptive Christian Ethics*, 117.

becomes so important for the privileged. Being part of the solution to issues of marginalization must begin with seeing not only the people involved and hearing their stories, but then uncovering the legacies of systemic racism and oppression and working in solidarity to change them in ways that benefit those without power and remind us all that we are part of a human experiment to love God and each neighbor equally.

How U.S. Culture Creates Problems for Marginalized People

The United States carries with it the weight of its own past, from its founding at the expense of the native peoples in the Americas, to its enslavement of Africans, to its current systematic exploitation and marginalization of undocumented immigrants and a great many others. There is a deep need to name these injustices, especially by those who are harmed. There is also a deep need for white, U.S. citizens to accept their heritage and complicity in such systems. The white citizen majority and its ongoing sins of racism, classism, xenophobia, and long-term mistreatment of people of color have created an entire nation upon the backs of those struggling in a supposedly "post-racial" America to survive, thrive, and have the same rights and privileges as white U.S. citizens. White U.S. citizens, myself included, have created and perpetuated evil in our society that needs urgent attention. We cannot in good conscience continue to allow such fear and systematic evil control our society. We must listen to the stories, the problems, the version of events in the voice of those harmed—and then we as the privileged majority must respond in solidarity.

Culturally-Produced Evil and
How to Religiously Overcome It

Emilie Townes, a highly regarded Womanist[2] scholar, argues that in order to define, engage, and eliminate the problem of what she describes as culturally-produced evil, one must enter into the interior parts of the lives of marginalized and oppressed people as well as the structures that put them in that position in order to have an "interstructured analysis that includes class, gender, and race,"[3] leading to a more comprehensive understanding of oppression and privilege. Her book *Womanist Ethics and the Cultural Production of Evil* provides a helpful discourse to "expose the ways in which a society can produce misery and suffering in relentlessly systematic and sublimely structural ways." [4]

Townes describes a "Womanist dancing mind," or a mind open and exploring the struggles, realities, and dangers facing those oppressed by the society around them. This dancing mind is not one that simply explains a generic situation of oppression, but delves instead into the particularities of a "particular community of communities yearning for a common fire banked by the billows of justice and hope."[5] Within this framework, she begins the work of understanding where these culturally-produced evil structures do and do not originate and how to combat them. She does this through focusing on the particularities of given culture(s) in order

2. Womanist theology relates to and departs from the work of Feminist and Black theology in that it focuses primarily on theology and religious practices as a framework to empower and liberate African American women and their communities in America. While Womanist scholarship is birthed from the African American tradition and thus focuses on the issues in that particular community as its prime objective, the scholarship is relevant to all women of color (and truly, any person of color) when applied in different circumstances. For this project, Womanist scholarship will speak to the reality and hardships of being a marginalized group of people in the United States. The marginalized referred to in this work are the undocumented immigrants among us, who have a similar set of circumstances leading to their marginalization.

3. Townes, *Womanist Ethics*, 12.

4. Ibid., 12.

5. Ibid., 2.

to explore issues related to gender, sexuality, sexism and to better understand where some of the systemic problems begin in cultural heritage. She describes the idea of "sites of memory" as her context in which to grasp the stories behind the institutional problems in order to get "into the interior worlds of those who endure structural evil as well as the worlds of structural evil itself to discover what truths may be found there."[6]

Her critical and analytical work insists that one cannot fully articulate or understand the structures of evil without examining the issues of class, race, and gender simultaneously—this is where the misery and suffering of structural evil is experienced in particular ways, with particular voices. She contrasts history and memory in interesting ways in order to bring about a new paradigm of understanding issues from differing points of view. To do this, she begins by decrying the comparison of history as objective and memory as subjective. The struggle with viewing history and memory in this way, she says, is that oftentimes the constructed "history" becomes a tool of oppression for those with the power to write history down, while the memories of those experiencing oppression are suppressed and forgotten. "Memory . . . is life, always carried by living societies, and therefore remains in permanent evolution, open to the dialectic of remembering and forgetting."[7] Memory, then, in some ways is more true to the experience of a culture than a reproduced history of a culture, and memories are stories told, not simply facts and figures reproduced and appropriated by a dominant culture. Townes says that "history usually becomes the terrain of Whites. It is objective, rational, and true. Memory is the terrain of Blacks . . . " (and I would suggest, many persons of color from a myriad of backgrounds other than privileged White persons in the United States) . . . "Memory is [seen as] subjective, emotional, and suspect."[8] Both history and memory are subjective, then and thus, both must be recognized for what they are and expanded to consider the diversities of others in order to

6. Ibid., 12.

7. Ibid., 14.

8. Ibid., 15.

create richer and deeper analysis of structural evil and the eventual changes needed to overcome it.[9]

Townes explores how structural evil can start with human life and cultures becoming "commodities that are marketed and consumed in the global marketplace"[10] through an in-depth look at how race and gender have been both ignored and used in cultural commodification. In the context of African American women, Townes uses various cultural descriptions of black women in America, beginning with a description of the Aunt Jemima phenomenon, which plays on white fairy tales about the black mammy, unsexed/plump/modest/older dark-skinned black woman, who supposedly thrived under slavery. She points out the many ways this image has permeated black lives and stories with a patent untruth about both age (most black women who worked in the home were young women), gender (most black women were not giving up their own children to raise their master's children in happy communion with the white family, but were coerced into sexual acts with white overseers), and race (most black women in the home were mulattas, or mix-raced, lighter-skinned women). Fortunes were made on the relatively rare "mammy" ideal to commodify racist assumptions and led to the belittling of marginalized African American women. The African American woman is by far not the only persona caricatured by oppressive white people, and Townes' work, while particular to African American women (whose ancestors immigrated by force as slaves into the United States), is relevant to the stories of *Mujeristas* and other women of color, which we have already examined.

Townes describes not only particular instances of commodification like the Mammy ideal, but also examines a force of hegemonic political dominion now led primarily by the United States (rather than Europe, as it had been in previous centuries). The United States has embraced this "city on a hill" status, providing a lighthouse of hope to the world for those who wish to remake themselves in a land of freedom, but it comes at a price

9. Ibid., 16.
10. Ibid., 3.

when dominant culture erases the intricacies of those who enter its lands. This master narrative of progress and hope is unfortunately mired in nationalism and ideological xenophobia (only our, civilized way is the proper way to achieve success, etc.) that has ultimately led to "an increase of political polarizations along the lines of nation, race, gender . . . class, denomination, and faith traditions . . . [where] culture is sanitized and then commodified."[11] She insists that in the case of race, white Americans too often create identity around what they are not—"not Black, not Asian, not Latino/a, not-Native American." Townes says that we must instead "be able to construct our identity, our selves, in such a way that we integrate the lives and histories of different peoples and cultures."[12] This is the only way to fully confront structural evil that arises out of cultural processes and understandings.

Rather than simply erasing the pleasing parts of the "city on a hill" myth for America, however, Townes suggests that we instead pay attention to "who and what may be at the foot of that hill (or clinging to its side) or to the cost we pay to keep our house on top of the mountain."[13] Only when we give space to those not benefiting from the myth can we begin to fully see injustice and work with those affected to create a more ethically sound society. We can then stand in solidarity, integrating others' voices with our own in order to create any kind of just society that takes risks to better the lives of all those living in community together.

Christianity has unfortunately also become a tool of commodification through its power in the political arena among those with higher standing, namely, the U.S. citizen white majority. Not only has it worked against the marginalized in very obvious ways (for instance, Scripture being used to condone slavery), but it continues to do so even as overt racism is less acceptable.[14] Townes

---

11. Ibid., 57.

12. Ibid., 73.

13. Ibid., 81.

14. Note: The rise of Donald Trump's 2016 presidential campaign revived the nationalist, misogynistic, and xenophobic culture, opening the door to overt racism against minorities (including the undocumented) once again,

describes this use of Christianity as "Christian triumphalism," an aggressive and domineering tradition of using Christianity to condemn some to hell and use the faith of a sinner as a means to overcome or triumph over sin. But this tradition often leads to a triumph over the non-Christian, who become the face of the devil, leading to persecution against their very being. This condemnation of "foes" against the grain of Christian "winners" leaves the national politics of the country (including its immigration policies) at the mercy of the imperial drive to control all those outside the hegemonic majority (white, U.S. citizen, and Christian), which Townes argues is antithetical to democracy. It is the work of the wealthy and powerful (read: white citizens with socially-acceptable religious preferences) to create hegemony in society (controlling reality and shaping it to please themselves), that ultimately ignores the real lives of millions of people who do not fit the mold.

Poverty, race, and immigration status thus remain off the radar of many in power, being chalked up to poor morality on the part of the marginalized. Townes aptly notes that "White power and privilege sashay[s] around with Christian triumphalism, empire, and imperialism . . . the elite White imagination creates a world complete with images built on stereotypes of utter otherness."[15] In the case of undocumented immigration, we are still in a time where undocumented immigrants are "othered" in profound ways, considered "criminals" for their very presence in the country, even as the outdated immigration laws do not offer enough recourse for

---

something many thought impossible after decades of improvement in civil discourse. At the time of this writing, in an early Trump presidency, many minorities and women are genuinely afraid due to the campaign's promises of deportation, as well as backlash by its followers, including white nationalist and other hate groups. I note the ongoing importance of protest groups such as Black Lives Matter, seeking to continue to uncover persistent racial disparities in the justice system and beyond, with the use of technology such as phone video recordings, as well as peaceful protesting. The political season of the 2016 presidential election reminded us and the whole world that the United States is far from racial reconciliation, thus this work of listening and solidarity must continue to be done for years to come.

15. Townes, *Womanist Ethics*, 109.

short-term workers or family reunification.[16] Until Christians can see fully the culturally-produced, evil structures supporting the marginalizing of people of color and undocumented immigrants, they cannot begin to break them down through political and social advocacy. Townes' explanation of the structures of evil and their origination points can help socially-minded Christians in position of privilege to see and then act.

To begin to combat such ingrained imperialism and othering, Townes posits that objective generalizations and observations are simply not enough to contend with the full reality of oppression and marginalization. Being a detached observer is not merely difficult, it is impossible. If one does not attempt to experience being the "other" through others' stories, one will only experience it from one's own social location, with all its biases and potential misunderstandings of what it means to be marginalized. Instead, there needs to be an emphasis on the context and experience of the marginalized to fully explore and confront the issues. She admits there are challenges this experience creates for analyzing, but she continues to insist that it helps us to "develop empathy and respect for others and, more importantly . . . creat[e] public policy, to share in the experience of others."[17] To fully examine knowledge claims, we must use the interconnected components of ethics, emotions, and reason. "As contextual, these components are often marked by class, gender, and race formations. When joined with religious values such as love and justice, these are powerful actors in public policy formation."[18]

We continue to perpetuate the supposed "Black woman's space" in society, just as we do the undocumented person's place. Townes says, "The damaging effect of such epistemological musings

16. Even those with immigration status, including some U.S. citizens, who happen to "look Arab," are treated as potential terrorists by some U.S. citizens, solely based on their cultural and religious heritage. This phenomenon is not limited to the undocumented, and is becoming more mainstream as the cultural backlash against a left-wing progressive Black president built as his presidency ended.

17. Townes, *Womanist Ethics*, 114.

18. Ibid., 115.

is that they take bits of Black reality and transform them into moral depravity as the norm for Black existence. This is structural evil working at its best (or worst)."[19] The reality for undocumented immigrants is similar—their existence in a country where they do not have legal status shapes how many of the privileged class (particularly white citizens) view them. According to a majority of far-right conservative politicians, undocumented immigrants are unworthy human beings, morally bankrupt rule-breakers, and obviously "out to get" white U.S. citizens and their jobs, healthcare, and social welfare.[20] The undocumented are thus hidden in shadow, for the white majority still needs their clothes laundered, their children cared for, and their vegetables harvested. They are simply ignored, until political necessity calls for a scapegoat to blame for whatever campaign promise is not being fulfilled.

This diminishing of an entire group's worth has led to the truncation of those lives at the bottom of the hill the city supposedly sits on. Townes rightly asserts that "public policies reflect the working out of our national value judgments. The moralization of poverty in the age of empire is a gruesome and death-dealing pageant for low-income and poor women, men, and children,"[21]

---

19. Ibid., 116.

20. See the Pew Research Center's data for polling related to recent deportation relief laws, noting that "non-Hispanic whites disapprove of it by nearly two-to-one (62% vs. 34%), with nearly half (49%) disapproving very strongly," "Unauthorized Immigrants: Who they are and what the Public Thinks," Pew Research Center. Additionally, Daniel J. Tichenor, PhD, of Rice University's Baker Institute for Public Policy has published a paper titled "The Congressional Dynamics of Immigration Reform," from the Baker Institute, which states, "border hawks today see the illegal immigration problem as nothing short of an unprecedented breakdown of American sovereignty that compromises national security, the rule of law, job opportunities for citizens, public education, and social services. Mobilized by conservative talk radio, columnists, and television commentators, many Main Street Republicans are outraged that the nation's fundamental interest in border control and law enforcement has been trumped by the power of immigrant labor, rights, and votes. Amnesty or legalization proposals inspire hostile resistance from this camp, which views them as unethical rewards to those who break the rules."

21. Townes, *Womanist Ethics*, 125.

and undocumented immigrants are no small part of this country's poorest and most marginalized. Townes calls for

> a more democratic epistemology . . . that stresses an interstructured autonomy, dependency, and interdependency [that dynamically] calls for a more truth-filled and more open process of making public policy decisions . . . a more inclusive epistemological stance in public policymaking [that] appreciates the diversity of our experiences rather than see them as nuisances or representative of special interest groups.[22]

She says that this different kind of approach would not necessarily start with simple individualism, but would instead begin with change to social structures that would enable all strata of society to work together to improve the systems we have. Townes would not begin this change from a purely "objective" standpoint (if there were such a thing). Instead, she would use religious notions of love and justice to claim rights as part of the assertion of our dignity and well-being. At best, this process is relational, not autonomous, and leads to a sense of caring that can be actualized for undocumented immigrants in accessible legal status and improved social standing.

Townes suggests that this change of structure must also occur on a religious level, or the church becomes (even more) complicit with the dominant political powers. If this change does not occur, religion sadly becomes only an opiate, and not a source of just change. She asserts that the notion of community itself must change. We must become more interdependent, focusing not on domination and competition, but on how we can better embrace the individualism of all persons in diversity: "it is not for us to garner absolute truth, but to be in a process of radical engagement with each other as we participate, together, in constructing the common good. This requires epistemological courage and theo-ethical fortitude."[23] Failure to do so leads to settling "for a weak

22. Ibid., 135.
23. Ibid., 136–37.

democratic system that runs roughshod over people is to reconcile with structural evil."[24]

Engaging this as a country, we use both intellect and emotion, in what Townes describes as a counter-narrative against the narrative of hegemonic imagination we all participate in daily. This kind of narrative will only dismantle systemic structures of oppression by "holding on to justice and peace as relevant, vital, necessary, and indispensable values that we can craft into faithful action in our scholarship, in the lives of those in our religious communities, and in the world we live in."[25] Keeping justice and peace at the forefront and listening to a diversity of particular lives, memories, and histories is ongoing work requiring a mediating ethic. Townes insists we should live "our lives not always comforted by the holy, but haunted by God's call to us to live a prophetic and spirit-filled life, and not just talk about it or wish for it or think about it—actions that mean that we remain in the tension."[26] We are to demand the uncovering of injustice and the working through of how we dismantle evil in order to meet the needs of those "least of these," including the stranger and the outcast.

But before we assert that the cultural production of evil and its hegemony sits outside of us, we must realize too that we are actually in a world that we helped to make, with those in a place of privilege having a great deal more work to do to overcome the poor imaginations we have had up to this point. All of us have better imagination deep within us. Townes says that, as black mystic and theologian Howard Thurman suggests in his autobiography *With Head and Heart,* we must blend head and heart to confront and change this social hegemony.[27] And, she insists, this must be a group project. There is no way to dismantle a cultural production without the work of community. "Individual acts, while helpful, will not provide enough moral oomph to unhinge and dismantle

24. Ibid., 137–38.
25. Ibid., 161.
26. Ibid., 161.
27. Ibid., 159.

the tremendously entrenched force of the fantastic hegemonic imagination."[28]

As the empire nation in a global world, those of us who are citizens of the United States have enormous influence on a global scale. We can do great good with our wealth and power (and have), but cannot fall prey to our own work ethic, only focusing on our insular needs as a bordered nation or our needs as the wealthy and white (and Christian). Part of Womanist theology and ethics is a deep focus on truth-telling. No longer do we simply believe the white myths about Blacks, Latinos and Latinas, or Arabs. No more do we amass power and wealth without digging up the bodies upon which the wealth is buried: "If we can hold on to digging up the truth when it gets buried in geopolitical, sociocultural, and theoethical cat fights and mud-wrestling contests, then we will be able to bring together justice-making and peacekeeping to dismantle evil."[29]

The real lives of people of color who must prove and justify their very being in places like immigration courts and ICE detention centers face challenges that white U.S. citizens cannot fathom. But Townes contends that this stuff of nightmares does not have to have the last word for Black women and men, or for any people of color or immigration status. Instead, she says, dreams can be more powerful than these nightmares and overcome through the intersection of challenge and hope. This challenge and hope come from those such as her Black foremothers and fathers who "refused to acquiesce to demonic stereotypes."[30] Townes says the hope given by them is also the hope passed on to future generations that bit by bit the culturally-produced evil will come crashing down. This combination of challenge and hope is what keeps the oppressed going when strength is weak and the present is discouraging: "This has the relentless and timeless force of water on the rock of the entrenched evils of the fantastic hegemonic imagination. Ultimately,

28. Ibid., 160.
29. Ibid., 162.
30. Ibid., 163.

the water wears the rock away through an unwillingness to alter its course."[31]

Living in this intersection of challenge and hope is not easy, for anyone. It requires living in the present and for the future simultaneously. It requires loving and caring for other people as ourselves and "interrupts the mundane and comfortable in us and calls us to move beyond ourselves and accept a new agenda for living."[32] This covenant commitment seems for Townes to mirror a marriage covenant—in sickness and health, in predictable and unpredictable, in safe and insecure. This requires a prophetic fury in order to protest "the sins of a fantastic hegemonic imagination."[33] This way of living requires what Townes calls "everydayness"—an everyday way of living faith deeply, recognizing accountability and responsibility for the justice and love that needs to happen in every facet of life, from personal to national to global. Townes tells us that: "The challenges of forging a tough solidarity demand all of our creativity and intellect as we step toward a more just and whole society."[34]

31. Ibid.
32. Ibid., 163.
33. Ibid.
34. Ibid., 150.

5

Responding Appropriately

RECOGNIZING THE STRUCTURES AND culturally-produced evil that white U.S. citizens have created is still not enough. White U.S. citizens will also need to recognize the personhood, rights, and autonomy of undocumented immigrants. Secular feminist scholar Martha Nussbaum provides a deeply thoughtful and philosophical reflection on what autonomy might mean for the most marginalized, especially poor women. Her work speaks well to the issue of the poorest and most marginalized undocumented immigrants, many of whom seek to be seen and heard as full persons in a society that has largely hidden them, ignored them, and given them no voice to speak for themselves.

Feminist Liberal Autonomy

A common critique of feminist thought is that it strays from liberal notions of rights and equality in favor of a general relativism. While certainly in some cases this may be true to some degree, other strands of feminism instead have reinvented these concepts of liberalism in unique ways that take into account the autonomy of the most oppressed women, as well as their resourcefulness and need for better social support as part of their community narratives. Martha Nussbaum in her book *Sex and Social Justice* does just that. She reclaims traditional liberal ideas of rights and autonomy for feminist thought. Instead of discarding extremely useful ways of approaching ethical reflection (such as individual autonomy and the function of universal goods), she reinvents them in feminist reflection on gender inequalities. She does not simply embrace the problem-ridden utilitarian views that often ignore much of the particularities of gender issues, but recreates Rawls' "primary goods" and "good functions" into "Central Human Functional Capabilities." Her capabilities approach moves from the focus on specific goods needed for human functioning to specific opportunities/capabilities needed for human flourishing. Flourishing, according to Nussbaum, moves beyond "bare humanness"[1] toward a life in which humans can fully function with dignity and choice. Nussbaum asserts that just because feminism so often looks at particular circumstances and relational collective flourishing, the work of liberalism is not absent, nor should it be, even if shaped into something somewhat different and more attentive to feminist principles. Nussbaum finds it intrinsically important for individual flourishing to happen first, before collective flourishing can. Women too often have been seen as means to an end and not ends in themselves, she reasons, and thus the individual approach of liberalism begins to move women (and I argue, any deeply oppressed group) from the shadows and into a place of importance.[2]

The scope of Nussbaum's work in *Sex and Social Justice* is broad and calls all societies and governments to task on the issue of marginalized women's struggles. While surely all governments and societies must work toward a more just system of moral and legal codes that address these issues, for purposes of this book, her work is useful in its focus on human dignity generally; that is, when discussing the millions of undocumented immigrants already in the United States. We must necessarily preclude extended conversation about their home countries and their shortcomings on human rights, though these play a deep role in the driving forces behind immigration, as noted in earlier chapters. Her

1. Nussbaum, *Sex and Social Justice*, 40.
2. Ibid., 62–63.

concept of human dignity is rooted in an approach that allows all people to flourish by creating and enforcing both laws and mores that guarantee a person's agency to live his or her life on his or her own terms. This approach provides space to discuss issues in various contexts, not just in the broad context in which she focuses. Undocumented immigrants lack much of what Nussbaum (and others) consider basic human rights that uphold their dignity as free agents and fully human persons. Nussbaum wants all societies to provide "social support for basic life functions, including prominently basic liberties"[3] for all human beings. While limited space forces us to forego the questions of whether and how home countries are failing or need to deal with these issues (one could write multiple volumes on the various crises in hundreds of countries globally), those same desires are being applied to a specific situation in which there are concrete ways for Christians living in a democratic society to enhance the life situations for millions of people by creating and enforcing laws and moral codes that create space for these persons to flourish. In other words, this book cannot and will not answer all of the global justice questions forcing or encouraging migration to other countries, but we will examine Nussbaum's capabilities approach to outline some of the ways the United States is falling short on treating undocumented immigrants with dignity, and it will provide some suggestions on how best to encourage privileged, white, U.S. citizen Christians to both understand and act on this issue.

Nussbaum's list of capabilities covers many of the needed abilities that must be addressed for any marginalized group, including marginalized undocumented immigrants in the United States. Some of the capabilities covered that are particularly important to the discussion of undocumented immigration include:

1. *Life.* Being able to live to the end of a human life of normal length; not dying prematurely or before one's life is so reduced as to be not worth living.[4]

3. Ibid., 20.
4. Ibid., 41.

For undocumented immigrants seeking new life in the United States, living a life of "normal length" is a constant struggle. Oftentimes immigrants die entering the U.S. through dangerous desert routes,[5] work back-breaking labor jobs for little pay for twelve hours a day when work is available, sending a great many immigrant men to their deaths.[6]

2. *Bodily Health and integrity.* Being able to have good health, including reproductive health; being adequately nourished; being able to have adequate shelter.[7]

Even if undocumented immigrants have made it into the U.S., their families are not eligible for affordable healthcare, and oftentimes avoid using healthcare facilities due to fear of providing damning documentation (or lack thereof) about their immigration status.[8]

3. *Bodily integrity.* Being able to move freely from place to place; being able to be secure against violent assault, including sexual assault, marital rape, and domestic violence; having opportunities for sexual satisfaction and for choice in matters of reproduction.[9]

Moving freely is not something undocumented immigrants do in the United States. Laws in states have become restrictive,[10] calling on local law enforcement to become immigration police, even as Immigration and Customs Enforcement (ICE) on the federal level has in recent years increased the number of raids resulting in mass deportations.[11] Without new laws to support their right to be pres-

5. Santos, "Arizona Desert Swallows Migrants on Riskier Paths."

6. Orrenius and Zavodny, "Do Immigrants Work in Riskier Jobs?"

7. Nussbaum, *Sex and Social Justice,* 41.

8. Tam, "What's Holding Undocumented Immigrants Back from Seeking Healthcare?"

9. Nussbaum, 41.

10. See ACLU, "Analysis of HB 56, 'Alabama Taxpayer and Citizen Protection Act'"; or See "State Laws Related to Immigration and Immigrants," National Conference of State Legislatures.

11. Gonzalez-Barrera and Krogstad, "U.S. deportations of immigrants reach record high in 2013."

ent in the U.S., undocumented immigrants will suffer from daily fear of being ripped from their families, jobs, and communities. Additionally, many undocumented Latinas use charities to receive healthcare, including many religiously-based charities that do not offer comprehensive reproductive healthcare, leading to a severe lack of choice on the part of poor immigrant women of color.[12]

4. *Affiliation*. (a) Being able to live for and in relation to others, to recognize and show concern for other human beings, to engage in various forms of social interaction; being able to imagine the situation of another and to have compassion for that situation; having the capability for both justice and friendship. (Protecting this capability means, once again, protecting institutions that constitute such forms of affiliation, and also protecting the freedoms of assembly and political speech.) (b) Having the social bases of self-respect and nonhumiliation; being able to be treated as a dignified being whose worth is equal to that of others. (This entails provisions of nondiscrimination.)[13]

Undocumented immigrants often lack any political or social voice, as they fear removal from the country as retribution for speaking out. Oftentimes in news reports and political rhetoric, undocumented immigrants are described in callous and nonhuman terms, degrading their very sense of self as they watch television news and read political reports from the state and national capitals. This

---

12. Recent pushback from various religious groups, including the U.S. Conference of Catholic Bishops has demanded exemption from dispensing emergency contraception or referral for abortion services. Reproductive healthcare is limited for some of the most vulnerable women, migrant women, some of them only children, many of whom are sexually assaulted and raped simply trying to enter the country. See Esther Yu-Hsi Lee's "Faith Groups Are Trying To Block Emergency Contraception For Raped Migrant Children." For the full written letter from the faith groups, see: U.S. Conference of Catholic Bishops, "Comments on Interim Final Rule on Unaccompanied Children."

13. Nussbaum, *Sex and Social Justice*, 41.

rhetoric can also move those who espouse the terms to violence and bullying of the undocumented population.[14]

5. *Control over one's environment.* (a) *Political*: being able to participate effectively in political choices that govern one's life; having the rights of political participation, free speech, and freedom of association. (b) *Material*: being able to hold property (both land and moveable goods); having the right to seek employment on an equal basis with others; having the freedom from unwarranted search and seizure. In work, being able to work as a human being, exercising practical reason and entering into meaningful relationships of mutual recognition with other workers.[15]

Aside from the obvious ramifications of being undocumented (being unable to obtain authorized employment, being able to vote in elections that affect their lives in the U.S.), undocumented immigrants often cannot obtain employment protections because they must work "off the grid" or use a fake social security number and identification to work, gaining all of the taxation without representation or benefit.[16] Additionally, working on or off the grid, these workers cannot make claims against unjust employment practices that U.S. citizens can because of their fears of deportation. Undocumented immigrants face setbacks to home ownership and banking practices (though this is beginning to change in recent years).[17] Also, undocumented immigrants who have grown up in the United States, brought here as young children, and having very few ties to their birth country, often graduate high school with few job prospects or struggle to get an education that will allow them to enter the job field. Even with a U.S. degree, this generation has struggled to find meaningful work due to a lack of status chosen for them as children. The recent executive action on immigra-

14. "Anti-Immigrant Hate Crimes," Southern Poverty Law Center.

15. Nussbaum, *Sex and Social Justice,* 42.

16. Francine J. Lipman, "The Taxation of Undocumented Immigrants: Separate, Unequal, and Without Representation."

17. Immigration Policy Center, "Serving the Underserved."

tion called Deferred Action for Childhood Arrivals (DACA)[18] has served to assist these DREAMers,[19] but with ongoing litigation against it and other executive immigration orders, they could again be in a precarious state of inability to work—and, even with a work card and job, these younger immigrants do not gain long-term status through their deferred deportation application. They are still at the mercy of restrictive, out-of-date immigration laws.[20]

Every group experiences these needs for assistance reaching their optimal capability in different ways, in specific contexts. This is where Nussbaum moves into a very concrete, feminist under-standing of rights and autonomy. Each capability she endorses (and the list above is not the complete list—there are many others, and even more she admits are not written in her book), need to be dealt with in different ways for different groups. For instance, in the case of undocumented immigration, simply providing blanket amnesty would not be a comprehensive enough solution, as other ongoing problems of racism and hate would still continue (as the United States learned with civil rights for black men and women), though of course better laws would be one, very large, required step forward for the undocumented. Certainly, with the capabili-ties approach, autonomy is protected, as each person still has his or her own choices he or she can make in life (which may or may not include everything on the list of potential actions one can take). But then they are no longer constrained by their inability to make those choices, which provides the space within which one can flourish in ways of his or her own making.

18. National Immigration Law Center, "The Obama Administration's DAPA and Expanded DACA Programs: FAQ."

19. Immigration Policy Center, "Who and Where the DREAMers Are."

20. "Deferred Action for Childhood Arrivals (DACA) is a prosecutorial discretion program administered by USCIS that provides temporary relief from deportation (deferred action) and work authorization to certain young people brought to the United States as children—often called "DREAMers." While DACA does not offer a pathway to legalization, it has helped over half a million eligible young adults move into mainstream life, thereby improv-ing their social and economic well-being," see: Immigration Policy Center, "A Guide to the Immigration Accountability Executive Action."

Solidarity and Risk for the Privileged

Once the voices of the marginalized are heard, their stories told, the socially-constructed evil unmasked, the importance of their autonomy recognized, and a lack of capabilities accepted as reality, white U.S. citizens then must find ways to move into solidarity with their undocumented friends and neighbors to begin the process of changing structures of evil perpetrated against them. Knowing the meaning of solidarity and the risk it entails is yet another way Christian feminist ethics can transform the way in which undocumented immigration is approached by white U.S. citizens. Solidarity is a word used in many contexts, but explored here is one distinctly liberative and feminist viewpoint from Rebecca Todd Peters, along with a discussion by Lisa Tessman about whether white U.S. citizens truly do flourish because of their privilege, and a description of the risks involved in moving into solidarity with the marginalized from Sharon D. Welch.

The Search for Solidarity's Meaning

Solidarity is not a term with a single definition. Rebecca Todd Peters in her book *Solidarity Ethics: Transformation in a Globalized World*, explores what solidarity might look like for the privileged through a lens of Christian social ethics, a public theology that "engages in critical social analysis . . . [to develop] normative moral criteria to help shape human behavior and social policy."[21] She layers on the work of critical feminist and liberationist theologies to examine "interstructured oppression, privileging standpoint theory and the importance of social location, and the emphasis on developing relationships across lines of difference."[22] She insists that *too much* focus on individual self-worth and dignity has clouded our view of the common good. While we should retain these affirmations of individual autonomy (as Nussbaum rightly contended), Peters says a theology of solidarity would go a step

21. Peters, *Solidarity Ethics,* 2.

22. Ibid., 3–4.

further, being "rooted in the values of mutuality, justice, and sustainability."[23] To create an ethic of solidarity, Peters proposes three foundations:

1. *Understanding social location and personal privilege.*[24]

Social location would include any identity-forming circumstances, including "race, gender, ethnicity, culture, sexual orientation, and class . . . that affect one's experience of the world."[25] We must go about understanding the social location we have individually and corporately and ask ourselves hard questions, "How does my ability to pay the bills each month cloud my view of what it means to be rich or poor?" or "How does my voice in a democratic society where I live and am in the majority change how I understand what it means to 'follow the law'?" or "How is my concept of God and my theology shaped by the way I view others in differing circumstances?" Only when we engage seriously the questions of where *we* are can we helpfully engage the social location of others in relation to us.

2. *Building relationships with people across lines of difference.*[26]

Doing this will promote long-term change through raising consciousness on a higher level than simply reading about others. It will eventually change the way the privileged understand their world by giving them faces, names, and stories—rather than being statistics on a page.

While reading this book will provide stories of immigrants struggling under the pressure of outdated immigration laws, the narrative of a person's life on paper pales in comparison to the lived reality of having a friend in this circumstance. As the story of Pablo showed, even those diametrically opposed to more open immigration in his community came around to better understand the plight of immigrants and their families (many of whom, like

23. Ibid., 7.
24. Ibid., 10.
25. Ibid.
26. Ibid.

Pablo's, are mix-status with a U.S. citizen spouse and U.S. citizen children) in ways we cannot by simply reading about them. Immigration is not an issue, it is a group of people with lives, families, and communities living among U.S. citizen families and communities. Without close daily interaction, we may never fully know what it means to be in solidarity.

3. *Engaging in structural change.*[27]

More than compassion as the sole religious response to suffering, the poor and marginalized need justice through structural changes to the social problems that ensnare them in cycles of ongoing oppression. Transformation of these structures can be addressed in many ways, but by far, religious persons have one of the strongest and most meaningful ethical foundations upon which to analyze, critique, and ultimately change the damaging social structures harming marginalized people (as Womanist scholar Emilie Townes already showed us).

Peters says that because solidarity in the first world (such as white U.S. citizens in relation to undocumented immigrants) begins from a position of privilege, the discussion must also begin there—at the point of understanding privilege.[28] First, Peters suggests that those in positions of privilege must work through what she calls "categories of moral intuition."[29] Moral intuition is cultivated as persons "negotiate complex moral situations that are new or unfamiliar."[30] This moral compass functions out of a worldview a person has, and it begins in a stage of *sympathy*, or feelings of pity toward an "other," which ultimately still leaves a sharp divide between self and "other." The second stage is *responsibility*, when people of privilege realize their own complicity in the systems of oppression, but at this stage, they cannot imagine how they might make a difference in such a system. Plaguing this stage is a sense of paternalism, or perceived moral superiority toward

27. Ibid., 11.
28. Ibid., 30.
29. Ibid., 36.
30. Ibid., 35.

the other. While responsibility does move persons toward an understanding of privilege, it does not solve the underlying problem: that the "other" is still separate, different, and somehow less than the privileged person. The final stage Peters describes is *mutuality*. This category equalizes the marginalized and the privileged through the "understanding that the well-being of all creation is interdependent."[31] In mutual relationships, persons of privilege no longer seek to solve problems for the marginalized, and they see that social location, and not inherent worth, determines the place in which persons find themselves. Solidarity is built on mutuality and moral equality.[32] Solidarity is not simply a category of intuition, though. It goes a step further, in a commitment to moral action alongside those who are marginalized:

> While some people may simply act out of their moral intuitions, a more morally responsible course of action is for people to employ their moral agency to engage in ethical reflection that can help people discern how God is calling them to respond in word and deed to the injustice in the world.[33]

Peters then proposes how faith can assist in the work of the responsible action of solidarity by describing how Christian solidarity will "negotiate the territory between pragmatism and prophetic vision."[34] For Peters, the work of the Social Gospel[35] movement and liberation theologies, founded largely in the twentieth century,

31. Ibid., 40.

32. Ibid., 37–41.

33. Ibid., 43.

34. Ibid., 51.

35. Peters describes the work of the Social Gospel movement like this: "The Social Gospel movement responded to the injustice and social inequality that resulted from the Industrial Revolution and the urbanization of US American culture by fighting for living wages, safety, abolishing child labor, and a shorter workweek." Ibid., 49. The movement was later seen as too idealistic to be practical; even as some of the goals set forth were met, the loftier goals of undoing all inequality and making a utopian ideal in inner city NYC, where the movement was founded, seemed too far out of reach for those in the movement or those watching it from the outside.

have functioned well as a prophetic vision, but their idealism need not be the practical end goal, even as they are both dreams about the human spirit and heart. Instead, she layers on a form of pragmatism that makes solidarity into what she deems "both a theory and an action" that is both a way of understanding the world and a way of living in it. This theory-turned-action describes a way of being for both the marginalized and the privileged that connects the two groups based on their shared interests, values, and goals.[36] Personally, I deeply believe the work of all theology and ethics must have a practical application to be meaningful, and Peters takes the time to process how we can move toward solidarity in ways that might initiate the slow work of real change.

Peters outlines her theological anthropology—that human beings are created to be in relationship; there is something ontologically important about living in community with other people.[37] With that as background, two ways she suggests ordering the world are through sustainability and social justice. These two work together, for sustainability requires people of privilege who would normally be consuming and destroying to live more simply, thus bringing them into better community with those who already do live more simply by necessity. Social justice follows suit—just as we care for creation in ways that equalize others with our privilege, we are challenged to also care for those different from us to ensure everyone's needs are met, just as Old Testament legal codes required of the ancient Hebrews. God's covenant with God's people after liberation from slavery leads to a more just society.[38] Additionally, in the New Testament, Peters points out that the concept of *metanoia* (or a radical transformation of heart, mind, and soul) describes what can happen with the privileged when they move into solidarity with the poor and marginalized in their everyday lives in different ways. In other words, the inbreaking of Jesus's way of living, in solidarity with others, changes people's innermost

36. Ibid., 51.
37. Ibid., 54.
38. Ibid., 58.

being, redirecting them toward others in love,[39] in stark contrast to the systemic evils produced by a hegemonic culture.

What differentiates solidarity from the concept of Christian "brotherhood" (which meshes people's differences into one group of Christian community), is that solidarity recognizes people's differences as meaningful and deeply important to Christian mutual love. Christians rushing to the concept of "brotherhood" (its patriarchal implications aside) often try to quickly *overcome* strife due to differences instead of slowing down and *listening* to those marginalized by their differences. In solidarity, we can still have a common cause, but we also are allowed to *see* and *appreciate* differences, listen to the marginalized and different, and grow and learn alongside each other. These new and differing voices that are suddenly heard offer new ways for those in privileged positions to be accountable to their equal neighbors. There is then a sense of compassion among the group that moves toward material realities being enhanced and improved by the small steps of individual action to the larger steps of creating change on a global scale.[40]

Learning of one's privilege is not an easy process. Peters insists that though some amount of guilt will inevitably accompany the process of solidarity, guilt is not a healthy ongoing feeling, as it can lead to paralyzing fear and disable those seeking to undo their burden of guilt: "Shame and regret do nothing to establish God's vision of right relation and justice in the world."[41] She says that while we cannot necessarily be held accountable for historical injustices, we are nonetheless accountable for how we respond to history and must work to change the structures and processes by which the injustices have occurred or are occurring. Peters says that when difference ceases to be a divider and instead becomes an "avenue for epistemological insights about the nature of humanity,"[42] the privileged will have the opportunity to see their advantages and those that others do not have and begin to cease

39. Ibid., 60–61.
40. Ibid., 63–66.
41. Ibid., 81.
42. Ibid.

talking and start listening, creating a more just and egalitarian community.

Whether Oppressors Really Flourish

As an aside to recognizing privilege, white U.S. citizens also need to ask if this privilege, though outwardly seeming to benefit them, really does provide any basis for true flourishing. Are the oppressive privileged actually flourishing, even as their privilege affords them luxuries the marginalized do not possess? Is privilege really "the good life," or is avoiding solidarity with the poor and marginalized actually causing the privileged to miss out on what it means to "flourish"? Lisa Tessman, in her book *Burdened Virtues: Virtue Ethics for Liberatory Struggles,* uses feminist theory and Aristotelian virtue ethics to rethink the "good life" as it is considered for both the oppressed and the oppressor. She has gathered research based in virtue ethics but focuses on the plight of the oppressive meta-structures in which we find ourselves (a feminist change of focus from Aristotle's original work). She discusses the brokenness of the oppressed, but she also lays groundwork for examining the moral brokenness of oppressors who *seem* to be living "the good life" or "flourishing."

Of particular importance for this work is her chapter "The Ordinary Vices of Domination"[43] wherein she explores how those who benefit from power structures are considered to be flourishing in ways the oppressed are not, and yet are still damaged by their inherent oppressive (uncriticized) way of being. She explains that the vices of domination range from overt social oppression to simple, passive acceptance of unjust privileges built upon those who are positioned unjustly below them. She suggests that while violent, domineering men who batter women are not widely believed to be flourishing, persons who have unjust economic or status privileges are believed to be living the good life, or the "American Dream":

---

43. Tessman, *Burdened Virtues,* 53–80.

> This group could include anyone from the wealthy
> capitalist who exploits the labor of working people while
> remaining unsympathetic to the hardships of their stren-
> uous, unsafe, or deadening working conditions, to the
> hard-working but fulfilled and well-rewarded member
> of the middle or upper class who resists redistributive
> measures that would equalize wealth.[44]

Tessman says that those who benefit from unjust systems may begin to flourish as they "become critical of their own social privilege
[and] . . . try to change not only structural sources of oppression
but also their own characters."[45] The struggle is real for character change, though, as Tessman points out that while one may
learn habits, such as no longer leaving the sidewalk upon meeting
someone different for fear of being seen as racist or classist, he or
she may yet continue in their fearfulness of the "other" on a more
visceral level. Much more work has to be done to effect character
change than simple changes in habits. The kinds of vices that continue in oppressively structured societies are so common Tessman
calls them "ordinary."[46]

Tessman argues that under virtue ethics theory, moral virtue
is necessary for flourishing, and those exhibiting the "ordinary
vices of domination" without critique are very far from the "good
life."[47] While the oppressors should not wallow in their brokenness,
which can lead to inaction, she does consider that "ordinary vices
of domination are all failings of other-regarding virtues"[48] and that
in Aristotelian ethics there is room for the concept of flourishing
"implicit in the liberatory goals of communities that are struggling
against oppression," maintaining "Aristotle's assumption that the
health of a social collectivity is key for any individual member's
well-being."[49] Oppression equally, but in different ways, affects the

44. Ibid., 54–55.
45. Ibid., 53.
46. Ibid.
47. Ibid., 56.
48. Ibid., 63.
49. Ibid., 75.

hope of both the oppressor and the oppressed for attaining the good life. Moral virtue must be understood not simply from an individual perspective, but from a collective perspective. The *polis* as a whole flourishes only as much as its members are virtuous, and leading a life of privilege necessarily precludes human virtue, as privilege is only apparent when society's members are leading lives of vice.[50] While the obvious damaging effects of oppression to the oppressed need not be outlined here, the strong word from Tessman is that we all will suffer if unchecked oppression continues under the guise of "ordinariness." Thus, we must step out of the bounds of acceptance into a place of solidarity and change. And this will require risk-based action on the part of the privileged.

Risks Moving Forward in Solidarity

Sharon D. Welch in her book, *A Feminist Ethic of Risk*, calls for an "ethic of risk" within the concept of solidarity, which she defines as "responsible action" that engages critically *with* (and not for) members of other communities.[51] She says that what those with privilege view as "responsible action" may have very little to do with what the marginalized and oppressed need or desire. Welch describes a different kind of moral reasoning, based in communicative ethics, that involves "accountability to others, an openness to critique and insight from other perspectives."[52] The risk undertaken in these kinds of encounters involves both the maturity to live among others as equals and not above them as overseers (community), as well as the risk to make mistakes and fail to solve all societal problems in a single generation (partial resolution):

> Responsible action means changing what can be altered in the present even though a problem is not completely resolved. Responsible action provides partial resolutions and the inspiration and conditions for further partial

50. Ibid., 59.

51. Welch, *A Feminist Ethic of Risk*, 16.

52. Ibid., 18.

resolutions by others. It is sustained and enabled by participation in a community of resistance.[53]

This moral action becomes appropriate to the needs of others not
only because of its immediate results, but also because of the pos-
sibilities it creates. One person cannot resolve other people's problems, but participation in communal work with others can provide
the necessary changes in systems that allow all parties more pos-
sibilities, even if it does not immediately resolve all problems in
the interim.

This feminist ethic of risk is a multilayered approach to both
ethics (a frame of morality) and a way of being (an action-based
lifestyle). For Welch, these two are inextricably linked. We must
first see the problems with our current approaches and understandings, then really see the people affected by those approaches,
and finally in solidarity, risk a great deal to move forward with
others into a new shared reality framed by justice. This ethic has
strong words for the privileged and provides a whole new framework from which Christians can work alongside others in oppressed situations, that ultimately can effect incremental change in
structures and systems that oppress.

Welch begins her argument by pointing out the ways in
which what she deems "the ethic of control" has dominated our
discourse and our political imagination as a Western society. This
ethic of control is so deeply entrenched in our cultural and political lives that we as Euro-American middle-class persons cannot
imagine another alternative. For instance, the "burnout" of white,
middle class persons working in social justice is based in this ethic
of control. Doing something in response to injustice becomes a
question of what "responsible action" should produce. By assuming we can "do something" to effect change, we continue the cycle
of desiring to control "events and receiv[e] a quick and predictable
response . . . we are shaped by an ethic of control—the assumption
that effective action is unambiguous, unilateral, and decisive."[54]

53. Ibid., 75.
54. Ibid., 25.

She insists the only way to begin to inch out of this ethic of control is to move into solidarity with the oppressed and *act on it*.

Welch provides specific descriptions of actions that those with privilege in solidarity with the marginalized might consider. Her description of how a feminist ethic of risk might happen theologically for those in solidarity is framed in the "beloved community," which "names the matrix within which life is celebrated, love is worshiped, and partial victories over injustice lay the groundwork for further acts of criticism and courageous defiance."[55] She describes a communicative ethic grounded in "dangerous memories" that drive the moral outrage and function to help create justice from remembering. Welch says this communicative life is not seeking consensus, but a "mutual critique leading to more adequate understanding of what is just and how particular forms of justice may be achieved."[56] When we critique our notions of what is just by recognizing our privilege, we may find ourselves challenged in ways that make us better suited to seek the right kind(s) of justice for those with whom we seek to be in solidarity. This solidarity with others is based on mutual love and a willingness to communicate in ways that allow for learning and growth toward equality. This mutual love is not a love of self-sacrifice, which is damaging to self-love (a deep problem among the oppressed), but a love that helps us to "accept accountability (in contrast to feeling guilt) and motivates our search for ways to end our complicity with structures of oppression."[57]

To achieve beloved community, Christians of privilege need to *really see* and live with the oppressed genuinely. This means not cringing at their anger or dismissing their feelings. It means not giving up on causes that support and change their lives, even when it makes us uncomfortable, even when it puts us at legal risk.[58] We

---

55. Ibid., 161.

56. Ibid., 129.

57. Ibid., 162.

58. "Sanctuary Cities," or places where immigrants are not immediately handed over to immigration authorities even if detained for other offenses, are one of a few ways localities have chosen to respond to anti-immigrant laws, but

need to avoid succumbing to what Welch calls the "middle-class numbness [that] is a luxury of being able to avoid direct interaction with victims."[59] Love is not just sacrificing oneself for another, but giving love in community out of abundance. The immanence of the divine in all things good and right, as well as the creative outflow of fighting injustice, is for Welch what becomes grace in community. She says, "grace is not the opposite of works; it is the gift of being loved and loving that enables work for justice."[60]

Her argument in support of an action-based ethic of risk does not initially lean on philosophy. Instead, she provides a litany of narratives, highlighting the struggles of those oppressed by racism. Her work *with* women of color (note again: not *for* women of color) strengthens her argument in support of an ethic that is broadly inclusive and constantly critical of itself. She paints a picture of white, middle class despair as inimical to successful work in social justice. The privileged cannot seek social justice very well inside an ethic of control without succumbing to the problem of cultured despair—because one whose life is not controlled by oppression (but indeed is bettered by someone else's oppression) will begin to despair over the ills of the world and lose sight of the work that needs doing, returning to her relatively easy life. She will not have what Welch calls the "rage" to continue the work. To have this kind of strength, it is essential that we become part of the lives of the oppressed, providing voices of defiance and indicting our own complicity in the imbalances of power.

Welch's ethic proposes three ways in which "to maintain resistance in the face of overwhelming odds: a redefinition of responsible action, grounding in community, and strategic risk-taking."[61]

---

in doing so, these cities and towns (and sometimes sanctuary churches, who choose not to cooperate with immigration enforcement) have put themselves at legal risk, from threats to arrest or sue, to withholding federal dollars from localities. Protecting immigrants from what cities or nonprofit groups see as unjust laws, can come with consequences. See: Cameron, "How sanctuary cities work, and how Trump's executive order might affect them."

59. Ibid., 168.

60. Ibid., 174.

61. Ibid., 46.

Her kind of responsible action begins in communal memory, formed from the defiant voices of the oppressed. She notes, "Justice cannot be created for the poor by the rich, for it requires the transfer of power from the oppressors to the oppressed, the elimination of charity, and the enactment of justice."[62] Risk-based action recognizes the limits of any given group to effect change. Without a doubt, voices must be strong and defiant, filled with a "holy boldness," but they also must be realistic and ready to take even small steps to make change a reality for future generations.

Welch then spends time indicting liberal and postliberal theologies for their shortcomings—whether too essentialist-driven or lacking the critique of power structures or misogyny. She instead evokes the deconstruction of the typical "eschatological reservation" of liberal and postliberal theologians, which says that all our good works are only partial, though nonetheless works with and in divine purpose. She notes this reservation is grounded in an ethic of control and will ultimately only lead to cultured despair, whereas if grounded in liberative theology, it can create an imaginative questioning of what the genuine limits in society are for change. There is no longer a "naturalized" limit based in a theology of control, but rather, there is a *pressing of limits* in loving community to combat perceived social constraints to justice. She says, "The genuineness of the limits facing a people can best be assessed from the point of view of love for people and from the perspective of those involved in concrete struggles to live with joy and integrity."[63] Only in sophisticated questioning of these limits can self-critique emerge, checking "against the idolatrous reification of any particular human project."[64]

Welch digs deep into African-American narrative, which contains these "dangerous memories" that provide a background for combating serious woes that continue for the oppressed. By incorporating a deeper understanding of black women's suffering, Welch begins to have authority to speak with them about their

62. Ibid., 51.
63. Ibid., 110.
64. Ibid., 111.

struggles under oppressive systems. Reading Welch both indicts the privileged and offers a risk-based ethic to stand in solidarity with women (and really, all marginalized persons). With this new ethic of risk, privileged white U.S. citizen Christians can begin to see how women, undocumented immigrants, and all persons of color actually feel in their oppressed situation, even as they seek to change those situations in profound ways.

Welch's version of eschatological reservation provides an "out" for those who have lost hope in fighting systems of oppression: "Sole attention to the failures in history can blind us to the partial successes; the realization that more is yet to be done masks the fact that some good has been attained."[65] This notion "cannot provide such resiliency if grounded in a contrast between human actions and divine power. If political programs are faulted for not bringing about the Kingdom of God, and if failure is seen as evidence of the folly of all human actions, the will for political action is destroyed."[66] By embracing this notion of eschatological reservation not based in an ethic of control, those of us in positions of privilege can move past our burnout, recognizing both the boundaries of human hope and continually pressing on those boundaries to bring about many smaller changes over time.

The maintenance of a liberative theology is not easy, however. Welch says, "one of the challenges facing liberation movements is the maintenance of love and solidarity in a form that enhances differences."[67] We must not write off or assimilate the "other" into our own programs (as Welch points out in her discussion of oral cultures and other tribal differences). Welch insists that it matters greatly who is speaking when it comes to matters of great moral significance. By thoroughly experiencing others' stories, the privileged can begin to appreciate our interdependence and begin to live fuller, more whole, lives as we struggle together to overcome racism, sexism, and classism. What grounds this beloved community and helps the whole group effect change is a spirit of love—not

65. Ibid., 106.

66. Ibid., 109.

67. Ibid., 145.

one of self-sacrifice, but one of continual giving from abundance by all members. Welch describes this love as providing "the resiliency of commitment, vision, and hope when efforts for change either are defeated repeatedly or are shown to be insufficient."[68] This ethic of "love for self and for others can provide self-critique and social critique without the enervating cynicism of the eschatological reservation."[69]

To get to this kind of theology of love, Welch employs a redefinition of god—as a deity that is no longer an absolute power that can corrupt by its very nature, but instead is *the* relational power. She says "the power of compassion is divine"[70] and "we participate in divinity as we delight in the beauty of humankind, as we rage against all that destroys the dignity and complexity of life. The ability to love and to work for justice is profoundly spiritual."[71] We need to "learn innocence" to avoid continuing the cycle of harms to others, and this is part of divinity. We as the privileged in American society have too long oppressed persons both politically and socially. In the case of immigration, they have been doubly oppressed—by both legal status and race (much as women of color have as well). Persons of privilege must work alongside these marginalized people in their social struggles, in beloved community, with the help of the relational god, to assist with the ongoing need for change in these lives. Feminists like Welch help us reimagine the deity as a supporter and lover of the oppressed, rather than a cornerstone of power for the ruling class. Certainly the need for a theology that raises the oppressed to beloved status is ever-present, and Welch's strong assertion of a relational god is not unheard of, having much support in Trinitarian theology.[72]

68. Ibid., 165.

69. Ibid., 167.

70. Ibid. 173.

71. Ibid., 172.

72. "To confess that God is triune is to affirm that the eternal life of God is personal life in relationship . . . . It points to experiences of friendship, caring family relationships, and the inclusive community of free and equal persons as hints or intimations of the eternal life of God." Migliore, *Faith Seeking Understanding*, 76–79.

Additionally, Welch provides ways in which the privileged can not only understand theology and community, but ways we can act—fighting alongside our friends of color when racism bares itself, from ballgame to work to marketplace to church to immigration court.

This ethic is a powerful feminist ethic, asking much of those in privilege. Welch makes the case that action in solidarity by those in power is the only way to create space for the oppressed, to hear and see them, and ultimately to work alongside them. This feminist desire to situate persons, listen to them, and understand them from their own point of view is complemented by a radical call for defiance, rage, and powerful love and solidarity as we risk our own privilege for the better work of mutual love and justice.

6

Conclusion

OVERCOMING DECADES, EVEN CENTURIES, of oppression is no easy task. It demands a great deal of work on all sides to bring to fruition lasting, positive change. It continues to require ongoing care and reevaluation. The work of Christian feminist ethicists opens a myriad of very lucrative pathways for better understanding the problems facing the marginalized and the realities those of privilege must overcome in order to assist in the hard work of change. As Traci West showed us, communication between interested parties is a must. Both the privileged and the oppressed must be active in overcoming debasing characteristics put upon the marginalized by society. Privileged, white U.S. citizen Christians must stop talking and start listening to the stories of those affected, for as Ada María Isasi-Díaz pointed out, God is revealed in the everyday (*lo cotidiano*) and in the emotions drawn up from the narratives told by the real people involved.

By seeing undocumented immigrants as persons, hearing their stories, and recognizing privilege, our society can begin to unpack how our own systems of economy, faith, and mores have created the monster that is culturally-produced evil. Just as whites have only begun to deal with the stain on their past and present that is racism, as Emilie Townes points out, so too U.S. citizen Christians can begin to "face our demons" and start to unravel the work of God from the unhealthy habits of our nation and first-world society. Supporting laws and cultural changes that re-humanize and give voice to our undocumented neighbors is an important starting point.

Public policy and church teachings are value judgements and must be held to the high standards of the hard work of solidarity. This solidarity begins with recognizing the individual dignity of all human beings, whether undocumented or here legally, their liberties being part of their dignity. Rebecca Todd Peters confirms that this recognition of dignity can then move forward toward relationship building between the privileged and the oppressed so that the risks of solidarity moving toward justice might be undertaken together in community. Until something like Sharon Welch's ethic of risk replaces our ethic of control, the privileged cannot flourish and live the good life any more than the oppressed can. We are all harmed by oppressive structures, as Lisa Tessman showed us, and unraveling them is one of the many helpful tools we have through the work of Christian feminist ethics.

Undocumented immigration is a complex and unwieldy topic that cannot be fully explored in any one written work. It is instead a lived reality, one which requires both theory and practice to support it as a means to end suffering, draw out the marginalized, and take risks to make major changes in an oppressive system of injustice. While feminism began and continues to deal specifically with the plight of women in various contexts, the whole of the feminist scholarly endeavor need not be applied only to one subset of marginalized people. As Martha Nussbaum points out, "one's feminism is not mere identity politics, putting the interests of women as such above the interests of other marginalized groups. It is part of a systematic and justifiable program that addresses hierarchy across the board in the name of human dignity."[1] The work of feminist scholarship in religious theology and ethics (along with some secular work) speaks volumes to issues of great importance for our daily lives, whether we are privileged white U.S. citizens or the most oppressed and marginalized undocumented immigrant. Building bridges in many forms—through information, story,

1. Nussbaum, *Sex and Social Justice*, 71.

liberty, giving voice, flourishing, solidarity, and risk will create a more just society in which all persons, of any color or immigration status, are given space to live with equal regard.

Bibliography

Altman, Alex. "In Historic Vote, Senate Passes Historic Bipartisan Immigration Bill." *Time*. http://swampland.time.com/2013/06/27/in-historic-vote-senate-passes-bipartisan-immigration-bill/.

American Bar Association. "Fight Notario Fraud Project." http://www.americanbar.org/content/dam/aba/administrative/professional_responsibility/notario_fraud_materials_combined.authcheckdam.pdf.

American Civil Liberties Union. "Analysis of HB 56, 'Alabama Taxpayer and Citizen Protection Act.'" Online: https://www.aclu.org/immigrants-rights/analysis-hb-56-alabama-taxpayer-and-citizen-protection-act.

American Immigration Council. "Giving the Facts a Fighting Chance: Addressing Common Questions on Immigration." https://www.americanimmigrationcouncil.org/research/addressing-common-questions-immigration.

———. "Deferred Action for Childhood Arrivals: A Resource Page." http://www.immigrationpolicy.org/just-facts/deferred-action-childhood-arrivals-resource-page.

———. "The DREAM Act: Creating Opportunities for Immigrant Students and Supporting the U.S. Economy." https://www.americanimmigrationcouncil.org/sites/default/files/research/the_dream_act_creating_opportunities_for_immigrant_students_and_supporting_the_us_economy.pdf.

———. "Understanding the Legal Challenges to Executive Action." https://www.uscis.gov/humanitarian/consideration-deferred-action-childhood-arrivals-daca.

Bacon, Perry Jr. "Trump Supporter Deeply Wary of Illegal Immigration, Syrian Refugees in the U.S.: Polls." *NBC News*. https://docs.google.com/document/d/1ie6fnUU_fKen2LDJs4Eq-EJhj75SjehMY-MEUYRg6jU/edit?usp=sharing.

Ball, Molly. "Why Would Anyone Oppose the Violence Against Women Act?" *The Atlantic*. http://www.theatlantic.com/politics/archive/2013/02/why-would-anyone-oppose-the-violence-against-women-act/273103/.

Berlin, Ira. *Many Thousands Gone: The First Two Centuries of Slavery in North America*. Cambridge: Harvard University Press, 1998.

Berman, Mark. "California Begins Issuing Driver's Licenses Regardless of Immigration Status." *Washington Post*. http://www.washingtonpost.com/news/post-nation/wp/2015/01/02/california-begins-issuing-drivers-licenses-regardless-of-immigration-status/.

Bretherton, Luke. *Hospitality as Holiness: Christian Moral Witness Amid Moral Diversity*. Aldershot, Great Britain: Ashgate, 2006.

Brueggemann, Walter. *Deuteronomy*. Nashville: Abingdon, 2001.

Cameron, Darla. "How sanctuary cities work, and how Trump's executive order might affect them." The Washington Post. Online: https://www.washingtonpost.com/graphics/national/sanctuary-cities/ (accessed 21 February 2017).

Carroll R., M. Daniel. *Christians at the Border: Immigration, the Church, and the Bible*. Grand Rapids: Baker Academic, 2008.

Center for Immigration Studies. http://www.cis.org/.

Congress of the United States. "Immigration Policy in the United States." *Congress of the United States Congressional Budget Office Report*. http://www.cbo.gov/ftpdocs/70xx/doc7051/02–28-Immigration.pdf.

Curran, Charles E., Margaret A. Farley, and Richard A. McCormick, S.J. *Feminist Ethics and the Catholic Moral Tradition*. New York: Paulist, 1996.

de Burgos, Julia. *Song of the Simple Truth: The Complete Poems of Julia de Burgos*. Willimantic, CT: Curbstone/Northwestern University Press, 1997.

de Vogue, Ariane and Tal Kopan. "New Trump travel ban order nearing completion," CNN. Online: http://www.cnn.com/2017/02/20/politics/trump-new-executive-order-immigration/

Ewing, Walter A. "Opportunity and Exclusion: A Brief History of U.S. Immigration Policy." *Immigration Policy Center*. http://www.immigrationpolicy.org/special-reports/opportunity-and-exclusion-brief-history-us-immigration-policy.

"Executive Order: Border Security and Immigration Enforcement Improvements." White House Press Office. Online: https://www.whitehouse.gov/the-press-office/2017/01/25/executive-order-border-security-and-immigration-enforcement-improvements (accessed 21 February 2017).

Federation for American Immigration Reform (FAIR). "About Us." http://www.fairus.org/about.

Gogolak, E.C. "Ankle Monitors Weigh on Immigrant Mothers Released from Detention." *The New York Times*. http://www.nytimes.com/2015/11/16/nyregion/ankle-monitors-weigh-on-immigrant-mothers-released-from-detention.html.

Gonzalez-Barrera, Ana, and Jens Manuel Krogstad. "U.S. Deportations of Immigrants Reach Record High in 2013." Pew Hispanic Research Center.

http://www.pewresearch.org/fact-tank/2014/10/02/u-s-deportations-of-immigrants-reach-record-high-in-2013/.

Gowan, Donald E. "Wealth and Poverty in the Old Testament: The Case of the Widow, the Orphan, and the Sojourner." *Interpretation* 41, no. 4 (1987) 341–53.

Groody, Daniel G. "Crossing the Divide: Foundations of a Theology of Migration and Refugees." In *And You Welcomed Me: Migration and Catholic Social Teaching*, edited by Donald Kerwin and Jill Marie Gerschuta, 1–30. Lanham, MD: Lexington, 2009.

Gulasekaram, Pratheepan, and Karthick Ramakirshnan. "The Law is Clear: States Cannot Reject Syrian Refugees." *The Washington Post*. https://www.washingtonpost.com/posteverything/wp/2015/11/19/the-law-is-clear-states-cannot-reject-syrian-refugees/.

Hake, Bruce, and Judy Hake. "What the Bible Really Says About Immigration Policy: An Analysis of 'A Biblical Perspective on Immigration Policy' and 'And You Welcomed Me: Immigration and Catholic Social Teaching.'" *Bender's Immigration Bulletin*. https://www.ilw.com/articles/2010,0114-hake.pdf.

Hoffmeier, James K. *The Immigration Crisis: Immigrants, Aliens, and the Bible*. Wheaton, IL: Crossway, 2009.

Horner, Thomas M. "Changing Concepts of the 'Stranger' in the Old Testament." *Anglican Theological Review* 42, no. 1 (January 1960) 49–53.

Immigration and Customs Enforcement. "ICE Investigations: Mission Roles in Multi-Agency Areas of Responsibility." http://www.fbiic.gov/public/2008/may/ICE_Mission_Roles.pdf.

Immigration Policy Center. "A Guide to the Immigration Accountability Executive Action." http://www.immigrationpolicy.org/special-reports/guide-immigration-accountability-executive-action.

———. "Breaking Down the Problems: What's Wrong with Our Immigration System." https://www.americanimmigrationcouncil.org/sites/default/files/research/Problems_and_Solutions_2010.pdf.

———. "The Comprehensive Immigration Reform Act of 2010: A Summary." http://immigrationpolicy.org/just-facts/comprehensive-immigration-reform-act-2010-summary.

———. "Just Facts: Basic Immigration Resource Page." http://www.immigrationpolicy.org/just-facts/basics-immigration-resource-page.

———. "Mission: About the Immigration Council's Policy Program." http://www.immigrationpolicy.org/mission-3.

———. "Serving the Underserved." http://www.immigrationpolicy.org/perspectives/serving-under-served-banking-undocumented-immigrants.

———. "Who and Where the DREAMers Are." http://www.immigrationpolicy.org/just-facts/who-and-where-dreamers-are.

Isasi-Díaz, Ada María. *La Lucha Continues: Mujerista Theology*. Maryknoll, NY: Orbis, 2004.

———. "Defining our *Proyecto Histórico: Mujerista* Strategies for Liberation." In *Feminist Ethics and the Catholic Moral Tradition*, edited by Charles E. Curran, Margaret A. Farley, and Richard A. McCormick, S.J., 120–35. New York: Paulist, 1996.

Jacobson, Luis. "Donald Trump: 'The Mexican government . . . They Send the Bad Ones Over.'" *PolitiFact*. http://www.politifact.com/truth-o-meter/ statements/2015/aug/06/donald-trump/trump-mexican-government-they-send-bad-ones-over/.

Lee, Esther Yu-His. "Faith Groups Are Trying To Block Emergency Contraception For Raped Migrant Children." *ThinkProgress*. http:// thinkprogress.org/immigration/2015/03/05/3627571/faith-refugee-contraception/.

"The Left's Secret Immigration Plan." *Fox News Talking Points Memo*. http://www.billoreilly.com/b/The-Lefts-Secret-Immigration-Plan/ 483540857061244168.html.

Leland, John. "Some ID Theft Is Not for Profit, but to Get a Job." *New York Times*. http://www.nytimes.com/2006/09/04/us/04theft.html.

Lipman, Francine J. "The Taxation of Undocumented Immigrants: Separate, Unequal, and Without Representation." University of Nevada, Las Vegas— William S. Boyd School of Law Scholarly Commons. http://scholars.law. unlv.edu/cgi/viewcontent.cgi?article=1827&context=facpub.

"Lost in Detention." *PBS Frontline*. http://www.pbs.org/wgbh/frontline/film/ lost-in-detention/.

Maccoby, Hyam. "Holiness and Purity." In *Reading Leviticus: A Conversation with Mary Douglas*, edited by John F.A. Sawyer, 153–70. Sheffield, England: Sheffield Academic, 1996.

Migliore, Daniel L. *Faith Seeking Understanding: An Introduction to Christian Theology*. Grand Rapids: Eerdmans, 2004.

Migration Policy Institute. "Social Security 'No-Match' Letters: A Primer." http://www.migrationpolicy.org/pubs/BR5_SocialSecurityNoMatch_ 101007.pdf.

Miller, Joshua Rhett. "Minutemen Project Ready to Return to Border amid Wave of Illegal Immigration." *Fox News*. http://www.foxnews. com/us/2014/07/13/minuteman-project-vows-return-to-border-as-immigration-influx-continues.html.

Miller, Patrick D. "Israel as Host to Strangers." In *Israelite Religion and Biblical Theology: Collected Essays*. Edited by Patrick D. Miller. Journal for the Study of the Old Testament Supplement Series, no. 267, 548–71. Sheffield: Sheffield Academic, 2000.

National Conference of State Legislatures. "Analysis of Arizona's Immigration Law." http://www.ncsl.org/default.aspx?tabid=20263.

National Immigration Law Center. "The Obama Administration's DAPA and Expanded DACA Programs: FAQ." http://www.nilc.org/dapa&daca.html.

Nelson, Richard D. *Deuteronomy: A Commentary*. Louisville: Westminster John Knox, 2002.

Nussbaum, Martha. *Sex and Social Justice*. New York: Oxford University Press, 1999.

O'Neill, William. "Christian Hospitality and Solidarity with the Stranger." In *And You Welcomed Me: Migration and Catholic Social Teaching*, edited by Donald Kerwin and Jill Marie Gerschutz, 149–55. Lanham, MD: Lexington, 2009.

O'Reilly, Bill. "The Left's Secret Immigration Plan." Fox News Talking Points Memo. http://www.billoreilly.com/b/The-Lefts-Secret-Immigration-Plan/483540857061244168.html.

Orrenius, Pia M., and Madeline Zavodny. "Do Immigrants Work in Riskier Jobs?" PubMed Central (PMC). http://www.ncbi.nlm.nih.gov/pmc/articles/PMC2831347/.

Peters, Rebecca Todd. *Solidarity Ethics: Transformation in a Globalized World*. Minneapolis: Fortress, 2002.

Passel, Jeffrey S., and D'vera Cohn. "A Portrait of Unauthorized Immigrants in the United States." http://www.pewhispanic.org/2009/04/14/a-portrait-of-unauthorized-immigrants-in-the-united-states/.

———. "Demographic and Family Characteristics." Pew Hispanic Research Center. http://www.pewhispanic.org/2009/04/14/iii-demographic-and-family-characteristics/.

———. "Origins of Unauthorized Immigrants: A Focus on Mexico." Pew Hispanic Research Center. http://www.pewhispanic.org/2009/04/14/v-origins-of-unauthorized-immigrants-a-focus-on-mexico/.

Pew Hispanic Research Center. "Data Trend—Society and Demographics, Immigrants." http://www.pewresearch.org/data-trend/society-and-demographics/immigrants/.

———. "Unauthorized Immigrants: Who they are and what the public thinks." http://www.pewresearch.org/key-data-points/immigration/.

Pohl, Christine D. *Making Room: Recovering Hospitality as a Christian Tradition*. Grand Rapids: Eerdmans, 1999.

Porter, Eduardo. "Illegal Immigrants Are Bolstering Social Security With Billions." *New York Times*. http://query.nytimes.com/gst/fullpage.html?res=9803EEDD1F3FF936A35757C0A9639C8B63&scp=2&sq=illegal%20immigrants%20taxes&st=cse.

Price, Michael and Falza Patel. "Muslim Registry or NSEERS Reboot Would Be Unconstitutional." *Lawfare Blog*. https://www.lawfareblog.com/muslim-registry-or-nseers-reboot-would-be-unconstitutional.

Pritchard, James B., ed. *Ancient Near Eastern Texts Relating to the Old Testament*, 3d ed. Princeton: Princeton University Press, 1969.

Runtenberg, Jim. "Bush Takes On Conservatives Over Immigration." *New York Times*. http://www.nytimes.com/2007/05/30/washington/30immig.html?_r=1&ref=business.

Santos, Fernanda. "Arizona Desert Swallows Migrants on Riskier Paths." *New York Times*. http://www.nytimes.com/2013/05/21/us/immigrant-death-rate-rises-on-illegal-crossings.html.

Sherman, Amy. "Donald Trump Wrongly Says the Number of Illegal Immigrants is 30 Million or Higher." *PolitiFact.* http://www.politifact.com/florida/statements/2015/jul/28/donald-trump/donald-trump-says-number-illegal-immigrants-30-mil/

Smith, Andrea. *Conquest: Sexual Violence and American Indian Genocide.* Durham: Duke University Press, 2015.

Soerens, Matthew, and Jenny Hwang. *Welcoming the Stranger Justice, Compassion & Truth in the Immigration Debate.* Downers Grove, IL: InterVarsity, 2009.

Southern Poverty Law Center. "Anti-Immigrant Hate Crimes." http://www.splcenter.org/intelligence-report/-year-hate/anti-immigrant-hate-crimes.

Tam, Ruth. "What's Holding Undocumented Immigrants Back from Seeking Healthcare?" *PBS.* http://www.pbs.org/newshour/updates/whats-holding-undocumented-immigrants-back/.

Tan, Michael. "President Obama Wants to Continue Imprisoning Immigrant Families." *ACLU.* https://www.aclu.org/blog/speak-freely/president-obama-wants-continue-imprisoning-immigrant-families.

Tessman, Lisa. *Burdened Virtues: Virtue Ethics for Liberatory Struggles.* New York: Oxford University Press, 2005.

"Texas: Judge Again Refuses to Block Refugees." *The New York Times.* http://www.nytimes.com/2016/02/09/us/texas-judge-again-refuses-to-block-refugees.html?_r=.

"The DREAM Act: Good for our Economy, Good for our Security, Good for our Nation." *White House.* https://www.whitehouse.gov/sites/default/files/DREAM-Act-WhiteHouse-FactSheet.pdf.

Thun, David. "'Notario Publico' And Notary Fraud." *National Notary Association.* https://www.nationalnotary.org/notary-bulletin/blog/2015/10/notario-publico-and-notary-fraud.

Tichenor, Daniel J. "The Congressional Dynamics of Immigration Reform." *Rice University's Baker Institute for Public Policy.* http://bakerinstitute.org/media/files/event/00794bd6/LAI-pub-TichenorCongressionalDynamicsImmigration-040813.pdf.

Townes, Emilie M. *The Cultural Production of Evil.* New York: Palgrave McMillian, 2006.

Turkewitz, Julie. "Immigrant Mothers Released From Holding Centers, but With Ankle Monitors." *The New York Times.* http://www.nytimes.com/2014/07/30/nyregion/immigrant-mothers-released-from-holding-centers-but-with-ankle-monitors.html.

"U.S. Immigration Since 1965." *History.* http://www.history.com/topics/us-immigration-since-1965.

United States Citizenship and Immigration Services. "Consideration of Deferred Action for Childhood Arrivals (DACA)." https://www.uscis.gov/humanitarian/consideration-deferred-action-childhood-arrivals-daca.

———. "New Design: The Green Card Goes Green." *The Beacon.* http://blog.uscis.gov/2010/05/new-design-green-card-goes-green.html).

U.S. Conference of Catholic Bishops. "Comments on Interim Final Rule on Unaccompanied Children." http://www.usccb.org/about/general-counsel/rulemaking/upload/02-20-15-comments-UM.pdf.

U.S. Department of State Office of the Historian. "The Immigration Act of 1924 (The Johnson-Reed Act)." https://history.state.gov/milestones/1921–1936/immigration-act.

U.S. Department of State Office of the Historian. "The Immigration and Nationality Act of 1952 (The McCarran-Walter Act)." https://history.state.gov/milestones/1945–1952/immigration-act.

Von Drehle, David. "The Great Wall of America." *Time*. http://www.time.com/time/magazine/article/0,9171,1816488,00.html.

Welch, Sharon. *A Feminist Ethic of Risk*. Minneapolis: Augsburg Fortress, 2000.

West, Tracy. *Disruptive Christian Ethics*. Louisville, KY: Westminster John Knox, 2006.

Wilbanks, Dana W. *Re-Creating America: The Ethics of U.S. Immigration and Refugee Policy from a Christian Perspective*. Nashville: Abingdon, 1996.

Wright, N.T. *Jesus and the Victory of God*. Minneapolis: Fortress, 1996.

Yu-Hsi Lee, Esther. "Faith Groups Are Trying To Block Emergency Contraception For Raped Migrant Children." *ThinkProgress*. http://thinkprogress.org/immigration/2015/03/05/3627571/faith-refugee-contraception/.

Zinn, Howard. *A People's History of The United States: 1492–Present*. New York: HarperCollins, 2003.